Cambridge Lati

Unit 1
Teacher's Manual

FIFTH EDITION

CAMBRIDGE
UNIVERSITY PRESS

CAMBRIDGE
UNIVERSITY PRESS

University Printing House, Cambridge CB2 8BS, United Kingdom

One Liberty Plaza, 20th Floor, New York, NY 10006, USA

477 Williamstown Road, Port Melbourne, VIC 3207, Australia

314–321, 3rd Floor, Plot 3, Splendor Forum, Jasola District Centre,
New Delhi – 110025, India

79 Anson Road, #06–04/06, Singapore 079906

Cambridge University Press is part of the University of Cambridge.

It furthers the University's mission by disseminating knowledge in the pursuit of
education, learning and research at the highest international levels of excellence.

Information on this title: education.cambridge.org

The Cambridge Latin Course is an outcome of work jointly commissioned by the
Cambridge School Classics Project and the Schools Council © Schools Council
1970, 1982 (succeeded by the School Curriculum Development Committee © SCDC
Publications 1988).

First published 1970
Second edition 1982
Third edition 1988
Fourth edition 2001
Fifth edition 2015

20 19 18 17 16 15 14 13 12 11 10 9 8 7 6

Printed in Mexico by Editorial Impresora Apolo, S.A. de C.V.

Library of Congress Cataloging in Publication Data

Data available

ISBN 978-1-107-67861-3

Cover image, © Ministero per i Beni e le Attività Culturali, background, © Semisatch /
Shutterstock

Contents

PREFACE

It is almost fifty years since the University of Cambridge School Classics Project (CSCP) began to research and develop *"materials and techniques which will accelerate and improve pupils' ability to read classical Latin literature and widen their knowledge of classical civilisation."* This Fifth Edition of the *Cambridge Latin Course* therefore builds on half a century of experience in researching, trialing, developing, and improving what is now the world's leading Latin program.

The *Course* was last revised in the late 1990s and the Fourth Edition has served teachers and students well for many years. A new edition will always present authors and editors with opportunities for development and change. On this occasion, following extensive discussion with teachers, we have chosen to:

- improve the physical layout of the material, increasing the page size to allow new vocabulary to be glossed alongside, rather than below, the reading passages. This layout has been found to improve students' reading fluency as it enables them to find glossed vocabulary more quickly and to return to their place in the reading material more easily;
- shorten the Course very slightly, primarily by gently trimming the reading passages, but also by occasionally removing a whole story, to take account of a slight reduction in teaching time;
- increase female representation within the story line, notably by introducing Lucia, a daughter for Caecilius and Metella. Where appropriate, the cultural material has also been reviewed to reflect recent research on women's lives in the Roman world;
- introduce color into the line drawings. Our aim is to portray more accurately the physical appearance of the Roman world and help students to realize that the ancient world was a world full of color.

Teachers who have used previous editions of the Course will note how heavily the Fifth Edition relies on the work done by earlier authors and editors. The previous work of Clarence Greig, Jill Dalladay, Roger Dalladay, Robin Griffin, David Morton, and Pat Story remains very much at the heart of this edition: most of what you will read, both in the student texts and in the teacher manuals, was originally their creation. Colleagues in the USA and Canada, particularly Martha Altieri, Pat Bell, Sarah Bjorkman, Ginny Blasi, Joe Davenport, Stan Farrow, Donna Gerard, William Lee, Clyde Lehmann, and Mark Pearsall have provided many insights, both into the development of the North American Fourth Edition and into the range of educational environments in which it is now used. It has been a source of great pleasure and learning to observe so many diverse and interesting lessons, from as far afield as Seattle, Boston, and San Antonio, and to talk with students and teachers in classrooms across North America.

Much of the work of the CSCP team takes place in a small attic in Cambridge, often quietly and usually without notice. It therefore gives me particular pleasure to have the opportunity to thank publicly my many colleagues who have together created this Fifth Edition. Ian Colvin, Martin Dawes, Christine Delaney, Bar Roden, Sukey Sleeper, Hannah Smith, Tony Smith, and Laila Tims have all played important roles in the revision process. Dr Maria Kilby deserves a special note of thanks for her careful research, particularly in the areas of color and female representation, her untiring attention to detail, and her very good humor over many years.

Special thanks are due also to Ben Harris, Classics editor at Cambridge University Press, who has gone far beyond the call of duty to deliver this edition, and whose patience and composure appear to know no limit. Few publishers would take the time to visit classrooms across North America, build real friendships with teachers, and understand their needs and their varying situations. Ben has done us a very great service and we are deeply indebted to him.

Finally, we would all like to thank the many teachers and students from around the world whose thoughts, ideas and experiences shape and inspire everything we do.

R. W. Griffiths, Director
Cambridge School Classics Project

SCOPE AND SEQUENCE

Stage	Name	Cultural context	Main language features
1	**Caecilius**	Pompeii; Caecilius and Metella's household; houses in Pompeii.	Word order in sentences with **est**. Word order in sentences without **est**. Nominative singular.
2	**in vīllā**	Pompeian daily life; clothing; food.	Nominative and accusative singular. Sentence pattern NOMINATIVE + ACCUSATIVE + VERB.
3	**negōtium**	Pompeian town life and business.	Nominative and accusative singular of 1st, 2nd, and 3rd declensions.
4	**in forō**	The forum at Pompeii: finance and the law courts.	1st and 2nd persons singular present, including **sum, es**.
5	**in theātrō**	The theater: actors and performances; pantomime, comedy.	Nominative plural. 3rd person plural present.
6	**Fēlīx**	Slaves and freedmen.	Imperfect and perfect (**v**-stems) in 3rd person singular and plural. **erat** and **erant**.
7	**cēna**	Burial customs; beliefs about life after death.	Sentence pattern ACCUSATIVE + VERB. Perfect tense (other than **v**-stems).
8	**gladiātōrēs**	The amphitheater and gladiatorial shows.	Accusative plural. Superlative adjectives.
9	**thermae**	The Roman baths.	Dative singular and plural. **ego, tū**: nominative, dative, and accusative. Sentence pattern NOMINATIVE + DATIVE + ACCUSATIVE + VERB.
10	**rhētor**	The Roman education system; books and writing materials.	1st and 2nd persons plural present including **esse**. Comparative adjectives.
11	**candidātī**	Pompeii: elections and local government.	Intransitive verbs with dative. Sentence pattern NOMINATIVE + DATIVE + VERB. **placet**. **nōs, vōs**: nominative, dative, and accusative. Different ways of asking questions.
12	**Vesuvius**	The eruption of Vesuvius; excavation of Pompeii and Herculaneum.	1st and 2nd persons (singular and plural) imperfect and perfect. 1st and 2nd persons (singular and plural) imperfect of **esse**.

INTRODUCTION

Why study Latin?

There are strong reasons for including Latin, particularly a reading course, in the curriculum:

Interest. Latin is intrinsically interesting to anyone who likes people, ideas, words, the past, or studying the way society works.

Understanding of language. The study of Latin provides students with an insight into the structure of an inflected language and encourages them to make instructive comparisons with the structure of their own language. In addition, they learn that many English words are derived from Latin and improve their command of their own language by adding to their vocabulary. Students also develop a sound basis for the study of Romance languages such as Spanish, French, and Italian, and an understanding of how these languages are related through their origins in Latin.

Literary appreciation. To develop critical insight into the way language is used to express feelings, to develop trains of thought, or to influence people, is a central aim of education. A reading approach to Latin has literary appreciation at its core.

Historical understanding. The period of the Roman empire is a key epoch of European history; it offers an excellent opportunity to learn about the past through primary sources in the form of written evidence and archaeological remains. Such a study promotes comparison with our own and other cultures.

Our origins. Through Latin, students gain insight into elements of western European and other societies: language, literature, law, attitudes to religion, philosophy, ethics, art, architecture, civil engineering and technology, and political science.

Careers. A knowledge of Latin facilitates the study of many subjects, including English, law, medical and biological sciences, history, and modern languages.

Objectives of the Course

The Course has two major objectives:

1   To teach comprehension of the Latin language for reading purposes.
2   To develop from the outset an understanding of the content, style, and values of Roman civilization, with special reference to the first century AD.

The Course presents language not as an end in itself, but as a means of gaining access to literature and to the culture from which it springs.

Principles of the Course

1   The Course attempts to present students with material that will engage and maintain their interest. Motivated students are more likely to make the effort to master the language and gain more knowledge and understanding of Roman culture and literature.
2   Language and culture are integrated from the very outset by using as much authentic Roman subject matter as possible. The Course is set firmly in the context of the Roman empire and frequently introduces historical characters. Its systematic presentation of

social, political, and historical aspects of Roman culture is both a valuable part of general education and an essential preparation for the reading of Roman authors.

3   Information about Roman culture is conveyed not only in the text of the Latin stories and the section in English in each Stage, but also by the large number of illustrations. These provide the student with visual evidence of the Roman world and are meant to be studied and discussed in conjunction with the text.

4   The Course draws a distinction between *knowledge about* the language and *skill in using* the language. Many students who appear to understand linguistic information when it is presented in isolation find it hard to apply that information in their reading. In the Course, reading experience precedes discussion and analysis. Comments on the language are elicited from students rather than presented to them.

5   Students are introduced from the beginning to common phrase and sentence patterns of the language which are systematically developed throughout the Course. Inflections and constructions are presented within these patterns in a controlled and gradual sequence. It is important that the students should understand the form and function of the words that make up a sentence or phrase, but equally important that they should develop the habit of grouping words together and treating the phrase or sentence as a single unit. Language learning consists of habit-forming as well as problem-solving.

6   The development of reading skill requires appropriate teaching methods:
   a)   Comprehension questions are widely used to assist and test understanding, and pave the way for the later approach to literature.
   b)   Translation is a most useful learning and testing device, but it is not all-important and sometimes can be dispensed with. The criterion for its use should be the degree to which it contributes to an intelligent understanding of what is read.
   c)   Vocabulary is best acquired through attentive reading and oral work in class, reinforced by review of selected common words in checklists.
   d)   Memorization of the paradigm of a verb or noun should not be undertaken in isolation. It cannot contribute to reading skill unless students also learn to recognize the function of inflections in the context of a Latin text.

Composition exercises from English into Latin do not contribute sufficiently to the development of reading skill to justify their inclusion in a reading course.

What do students gain?

The *CLC* can be taught to a wide ability range. Students who complete only Units 1 and 2 still gain an increased understanding of language and an awareness of the Roman contribution to western civilization. Those who complete Units 3 and 4 will be able to show understanding of an unprepared passage of level-appropriate Latin. They will have studied some Roman literature, both prose and verse, and will be able to make an informed response to the content, language, literary qualities, and cultural themes. They will also have studied aspects of Roman civilization occurring in the Course and in the literature, and will be able to appreciate the nature of historical and other evidence, and make comparisons between ancient and modern times.

Content of the Course

The students' material consists of Units (books) divided into Stages (chapters). Unit 1, set in Pompeii in the first century AD, is based on the **familia** of Lucius Caecilius Iucundus, whose house and business records survive; Unit 2 introduces two very different provinces of the Roman empire, Britain and Egypt; Unit 3 returns to Britain before taking us to the city of Rome; Unit 4 remains in Rome and focuses on life in the imperial court, before progressing to adapted and original literature.

Each Stage contains new language features and deals with a particular aspect of Roman culture; there is, in most cases, a standard format.

Model sentences. New language features are presented in a coherent context of whole sentences or short paragraphs, accompanied by line drawings.

Latin stories. Narrative and dramatic passages form the core of each Stage. They have a developing story line, and a context related to the aspect of Roman culture featured in the Stage. They are the main means of consolidating the language, and increase in length and complexity as the Course advances. New vocabulary is given alongside, in the form in which it appears in the text.

About the language. An explanation is provided of language features that have been introduced or have occurred frequently in the Stage. It usually appears some way into the Stage. It is designed to be studied after students have become familiar with the language features through the reading and investigation of the stories.

Practicing the language. Exercises consolidate important features of language which have been introduced in the current Stage or encountered previously.

Cultural context material. This provides an explanation of the aspect of Roman culture featured in the Stage and forms the context or subject matter of the Latin stories. It may contain extracts from Roman writers or archaeological findings and is copiously illustrated.

Vocabulary checklist. At the end of each Stage there is a list of common words which have occurred several times in the text and should now be known. In the early Stages, nouns and adjectives are presented in the nominative singular, and verbs in the 3rd person singular of the present tense. The Course gradually brings in the traditional key grammatical forms until finally the principal parts of verbs, the three genders of adjectives, and the genitive and gender of nouns are listed. Students are thus equipped to use a Latin dictionary.

Language information. This section at the end of each Unit summarizes the language content of the Unit; in Units 2–4 it also builds on the language features encountered in previous Units. It contains grammatical charts, notes, additional exercises, and a general vocabulary.

Supplementary materials

The Course website (www.CambridgeLatinCourse.com) provides a wide range of material to support the Course, including:

- interactive editions of the Latin stories, for use by students when reading individually or in pairs, or to allow the teacher to display the story to the whole class;
- audio recordings of the Latin stories;
- interactive language manipulation activities;
- digital vocabulary drills;

- digital dictionaries;
- printable study sheets to support the study of the stories, the language features, and the cultural topics;
- weblinks to enable further investigation of the cultural topic of each Stage.

Course planning

You need to build balance, pace, variety, and progression into the Course in order to help students achieve their highest level of success.

1   It is important to plan the whole Course in advance, identifying targets and drawing up a timetable. Remember that the grammatical gradient of the Course is spread over all four Units and that students have not completed their study of basic grammar until the end of Unit 4.

Each Unit of the Course is a carefully constructed program of study in its own right. Its ending is designed to ensure that students who do not continue with their study of Latin receive a meaningful conclusion to their learning. Therefore you should plan to finish each teaching year at the end of a Unit if at all possible.

A suggested plan for teaching the entire Course in high school is as follows:

Latin I: Units 1 and 2
Latin II: Unit 3
Latin III: Unit 4

After completing Unit 4, classes should be ready to start reading authors of their choice, or to follow the Advanced Placement syllabus.

For teachers who have a three-year program only, it is possible to finish Unit 3 and begin Unit 4 in the second year. Latin III would then start by finishing Unit 4, and at least the second half of the year could be used for reading chosen authors or selections.

In junior high or middle school, the Latin I curriculum could be spread over two years:

Seventh Grade: Unit 1
Eighth Grade: Unit 2

A suggested plan for teaching the Course in college or university is to complete Units 1–4 in the Freshman Year.

2   Whatever the length of your course, you should regularly include elements of: story line, linguistic material, cultural and historical content, teacher-aided reading with discussion to develop literary response, and independent reading of the easier stories.

3   Give students an exercise in translation or comprehension on a regular basis, as homework or classwork. The latter has the advantage that you can monitor students' progress directly and give help as needed. Use stories in the Course so that the overall story line (and therefore students' motivation) is maintained.

4   Plan allocations of time for systematic review. Ensure that you build in both formative and summative evaluation.

5   Some stories will have to be omitted by those moving quickly through the Course, e.g.:

Stage 3   **in forō** (p. 28)
Stage 4   Exercise 2, **Grumiō et leō** (p. 47)
Stage 5   Exercise 3, **in theātrō** (p. 63)

6   You will need to fill in the gaps for the class, in both language and story line. For example, translate the whole story to the class, keeping them involved by giving them the occasional word or phrase to translate or by asking them comprehension questions. ** before the title of a story in this manual indicates a story which may be omitted in the interests of time.

7   Stick to your timetable, even if it requires further cuts if necessary, so that the end of the academic year coincides with the end of a Unit. As a rough guide, each Stage of Unit 1 should require approximately three or four hours of classroom teaching time. Stages 1 and 2 are shorter and will therefore require less time.

8   Give students their own copy of the overall timetable for the Course so that they can be partners in keeping up the pace, and gain motivation from noting their progress. They should also be given a more detailed timetable for each semester.

Teaching method

The suggestions below are based on the principles of the Course, and offer a starting point from which you can develop strategies of your own according to the needs of your students.

Model sentences. A sequence for handling the model sentences might be:

1   Set the scene so that the students begin to understand the cultural context of the new Stage. This can be done by:
   a) a brief discussion of the picture on the title page
   b) quick reference to the line drawings
   c) introducing the cultural context material during a previous lesson or assigning it as homework.

2   Read aloud a group of sentences in Latin, slowly enough to be clear and distinct, and give students time to understand them.

3   Ask questions in English, carefully designed to elicit correct, concrete answers, in the order of the information in the Latin sentence, e.g. **spectātōrēs in theātrō sedent** (p. 56):

Q.	Who are in the picture?	A.	Spectators.
Q.	Where are they?	A.	In the theater.
Q.	Are they standing, walking, or sitting?	A.	Sitting.
Q.	So what does the whole sentence mean?	A.	The spectators are sitting in the theater.

4   Pass quickly on to the next sentence or group of sentences. Allow the students to discover the sense of the new feature for themselves, without explanation from you. The linguistic context and the line drawings usually provide sufficiently strong clues

so that the students often arrive at the right meaning after the first or second example. (Very often, by means of the inductive method outlined here, students will have correctly understood the new phenomenon before reading the About the language section.)

5 If a sentence has proved confusing, repeat it before moving on. Otherwise, sustain momentum by a quick pace of question and answer, and a swift transition from one sentence to the next.

6 A second run-through of all the sentences is advisable, perhaps at the beginning of the next lesson.

The Latin stories. These form a large part of each Stage and variety of approach is essential.

1 *Planning*:
   a) Divide a story into sections to be handled one at a time. Make sure the divisions are not arbitrary, but that each section makes sense in itself. Occasionally the class may be divided into groups, each of which (given a rough idea of the story line) prepares a different section of the story for the rest of the class.
   b) Different parts of a story may present varying levels of difficulty, and so need varying treatment, e.g.:
      Easy paragraphs: Read aloud in Latin, ask students to study the paragraph in pairs or groups, and check their understanding by asking comprehension questions; or ask students to explore individually, and then translate orally.
      Difficult paragraphs: Read aloud in smaller sections. Ask the whole group to suggest the meaning of individual words or phrases, gradually building up collectively the meaning of sentences and eventually the paragraph. Alternatively, read aloud with pauses to ask more knowledgeable students the meaning of key words or phrases. Groups then explore the passage. Use comprehension questions to advance the groups' understanding; follow up with translation.
   c) Similarly, in reading easy stories, students can work independently, whereas more guidance will be needed with difficult stories.

2 *Introducing a story*. Possible strategies include:
   a) *Looking back*. Reviewing a previous story, possibly anticipating how particular characters may react, or highlighting elements of the plot that are left unresolved.
   b) *Visual stimulus*. Discussing illustrations or showing images to present the visual setting.
   c) *Aural stimulus*. Reading the story aloud in a lively and dramatic manner (or playing a recorded reading) while students follow the text, gleaning some hints of the plot.
   d) *Looking forward*. Raising questions to which the students will discover answers.

3 *The first reading*. Here the aim is to establish the general sense.
   a) Read the first section of the story aloud in Latin, with the students following the text. It is essential that students are introduced to a passage by hearing it read aloud well. When they hear the words organized into phrases or clauses, and the characters differentiated, they glean some clues to the meaning. They should regularly read the Latin aloud themselves, observing phrase and clause boundaries.

b) Give the students time to study the text for themselves, using the vocabulary and any other help available. It is important to provide a supportive context that maximizes the chances of success. Sometimes organize the students in groups or pairs so that they can help each other. The teacher should circulate, giving encouragement and help, and noting on the board any points that will later need clarification.

With straightforward passages, students may be briefed from the outset to demonstrate their understanding in different ways by producing, e.g.:

- A summary of the main points (written or oral).
- An oral or written translation.
- A chart, map, or drawing for a topographical passage.
- A mime or a play of the incident described.
- A sequence of drawings to illustrate the sequence of events.

c) Check students' understanding by asking for feedback from the groups or by conducting a question and answer session. For example, questions on the first paragraph of **Fēlīx** (Stage 6, p. 72) might include:

Where were the Pompeians?

What were they doing?

Were there many or few Pompeians in the inn?

What did Clemens do?

Whom did Clemens see? How did he greet him? What does this suggest about their relationship?

Fēlīx erat lībertus. What does **lībertus** mean? What does it tell us about Felix?

d) Diagnose the source of any difficulties by taking the class slowly through problem sentences. Distinguish between uncertainty caused by forgetting the meaning of words, and failure to understand a relatively new language feature, e.g. omission of subject, apposition, or subordinate clause.

e) Work on any difficulties. The purpose of the first reading is to understand the meaning of the Latin, not to analyze the language. Two techniques are especially useful:

- Rephrasing or expanding questions to enable students to understand the Latin for themselves, e.g. (for the first paragraph of **Fēlīx**):

  Who were the people in the inn? Who came into the inn?

- Taking the students back to a model sentence with a familiar feature. Students recognize the model sentences and will quickly work out the similarity of the new context.

f) Oral or written translation can be useful to the teacher in checking and enhancing students' understanding of what has been read. It is best used after several sentences, or a whole paragraph, have been explored. It can be omitted for stories which the class have readily understood or explored intensively in other ways.

Initially, students may find it helpful to use a literal translation or a formula, e.g. using "was/were -ing" to translate the imperfect. The students themselves usually discover quite soon that, rather than a word-for-word process, translation involves rendering Latin into good English, in the appropriate register, so as to convey fully the original writer's meaning. It is the teacher's task to encourage them toward flexibility and the appropriate use of idiomatic phrases.

There is a variety of methods that can be used in classroom translation, e.g.:

- Each sentence is translated by a different student.
- One student translates a paragraph, others suggest improvements.
- Students work in pairs or groups.
- Students contribute suggestions for a collective class translation.

4   *Consolidation*: A follow-up is essential to strengthen and maintain the students' grasp of story, language, and cultural context, and to develop confidence and fluency in reading. Rereading should be as varied as possible and might include activities such as:

a)   *Listening and understanding.* Listen, with the book closed, to a reading by the teacher or from the software. Pause at strategic points to check understanding of the passage. Alternatively, students may mime to a Latin reading.

b)   *Latin reading.* Read the story aloud in Latin, with individuals or groups taking different parts or paragraphs. This could be presented to the class or recorded. Choral reading (the class together or in groups) encourages the less confident.

c)   *Discussion.* Bring out character, situation, cultural context.

d)   *Character analysis.* Foretell the actions or responses of certain characters in certain situations or "hot-seat" a main character. A well-informed student, or another teacher, takes on a character and sits in the center of the group to be questioned intensively about his or her motivation and feelings in a given situation.

e)   *Language practice.* Ask ten quick language questions at the end of a story (ten vocabulary items, ten verbs in a particular tense, etc.). Alternatively, isolate key phrases or sentences illustrating a new language feature; ask for meaning or ask students to copy them out, translate them, and keep for reference.

f)   *Retelling the story.* Tell the story from the viewpoint of one of the characters, taking care to bring out the personality and background details in the narrative; or tell it for a particular audience, e.g. for a seven-year-old, selecting appropriate vocabulary for the target audience.

g)   *Plot analysis.* Search for clues about how the story will continue next time. Speculate about the subsequent episode(s) in the "soap opera." Students enjoy outguessing the authors of the stories.

h)   *Cultural research.* Find out more about the most important places or processes contained in the story. This can lead to a retelling of the story with full descriptions and explanations.

i)   *Illustration.* Produce a picture which shows accurately the characters and their status, with details to establish their locations and the event(s) described. A correct comprehension of the language and the cultural context, rather than skill in drawing, is what matters here.

j)   *Games.* Conduct class competitions where students identify characters via Latin clues, arrange Latin story events in the correct sequence, etc.

k)   *Drama.* Act, read, or record in Latin, or by using an idiomatic translation.

l)   *Creative writing.* Retell the story from the viewpoint of one of the characters, continue the story, produce a diary entry or a journalistic article, write limericks or evocative poetry, etc.

m)   *Worksheets.* Indicate comprehension by answering true/false questions, doing multiple choice exercises, filling in blanks from a word bank, completing cloze exercises, etc.

n) *Translation.* Submit, on a regular basis, a polished translation of a prepared passage. This may be done in class or for homework. Students, individually or in groups, attempt to achieve the closest and most natural English version, perhaps of a dramatic scene for acting. Occasionally ask students to review a story carefully at home; tell them that you will give them three or four sentences from the story to translate in class without any help. This is a very precise check on understanding and is easy to set up and assess.

Working on the language. Students gain considerable linguistic understanding from the stories, but the Course provides reinforcement in specific ways.

About the language. In discussing a language feature, the teacher should:

1   Use the examples the students have already met in the model sentences and reading passages, in order to organize and consolidate the perceptions they are already forming.

2   Elicit comments on the language feature from the students themselves, rather than presenting the teacher's comment and explanation.

3   Use the practice examples in the About the language section to make sure that students have understood the explanation. If necessary, supplement these examples with others from the text.

4   Resist the temptation to take the discussion any further, since considerable experience in reading is necessary for students to reach a fuller understanding.

A possible discussion for the dative case (Stage 9) might go as follows.

Start by putting the model sentence **Clēmēns puellae vīnum offerēbat** on the board.

Q. What did we decide was the English meaning for this sentence?	A. Clemens was offering wine to the girl.
Q. Who did the offering?	A. Clemens.
Q. So what case is the Latin noun **Clēmēns**?	A. Nominative.
Q. And what was Clemens offering?	A. Wine.
Q. So what case is the Latin noun **vīnum**?	A. Accusative.
Q. To whom did Clemens offer the wine?	A. The girl.
Q. Where is the word for "to" in the Latin sentence?	A. There isn't one.

At this point, some students may be able to suggest that this new form **puellae** handles the idea of "to." Or the translation "Clemens was offering the girl wine" may have been given, without the "to." Either way, try to elicit from the students their understanding of "what is new" in Stage 9 before you give them the label "dative." You should give other examples, including those with the English equivalent "for," to build up students' concept of how English translations handle the Latin dative.

Practicing the language. Most of the exercises require students to complete sentences from a pool of words or phrases and are suitable for both oral and written work. In oral practice, students should respond with the complete Latin sentence, demonstrating their understanding by translating it or answering a question about its meaning.

Other exercises in this section include short stories to be tested by translation or comprehension questions. The level of difficulty is usually slightly below that of the other stories in the Stage.

Additional exercises. The Course is designed with built-in consolidation, and students will automatically meet further examples of a feature in later reading passages and exercises. However, teachers can easily give supplementary language practice. Possibilities include:

1 Using a story just read for reviewing a language feature or a range of features. This ensures that students study words and inflections in the context of a coherent narrative or conversation. Possible techniques are:

   a) *Search-and-find.* Have students identify examples of, for instance, the perfect and imperfect tenses or nominative and accusative noun forms, etc.

   b) *Oral substitution.* From **portābant** ask for the meanings of **portābat**, **portābam**, progressing to **portāvērunt**, **portant**, then to **portāvit**, **portō**, etc. The progression from easy to more difficult questions should be a gradual one. In the example given, first the person is changed, then the tense, then both variables.

   c) *Line-by-line questions*, sometimes followed up by a question designed to stress the link between form and function, e.g.:
   - In line 1, what tense is **ambulābant**? (And how is it translated?)
   - In line 2, is **dominō** singular or plural? (How does this affect translation?)
   - In line 3, find an accusative. (Why is the accusative being used?)

2 Listening to a brief, familiar passage read in Latin, with the textbook closed; students answer comprehension questions or translate sentence by sentence, or explain selected phrases. This should be done only with a story just studied or an easy story read previously.

3 Dictation of a brief Latin passage to consolidate grasp of sentence structure and to relate the spoken to the written word.

4 Memorization of a short piece of Latin text, e.g. a few model sentences, or three or four sentences in a story which contain key vocabulary or sentence structures.

Vocabulary checklist. The words in this list should already be familiar to students. They should be reviewed and tested. Frequent short vocabulary quizzes may help more than long ones at greater intervals. As you quiz or test students on their knowledge of the vocabulary words, you may vary the form of the word you present, but we would suggest that you require only the basic meaning when only vocabulary knowledge is being tested; e.g. recognition of a verb form as present or perfect is a grammar skill rather than a vocabulary skill, and should be quizzed or tested when grammar, rather than vocabulary, is the focus.

Discuss different ways of active learning with the class. Students may need reminding to cover up the English when studying, or to make flashcards. However, acquisition and retention of vocabulary depend largely upon the level of interest a story evokes and the frequency and variety of reinforcement activities, e.g.:

1 From a story just read ask the students to give the meaning of individual words, or short phrases, *with books open and glossary covered.*

2 *With books shut*, ask a series of questions about the story, setting selected words in a helpful context:

   The citizens were **laetī**. What mood were they in?

   Each supporter received a **fūstis**. What was that?

   Who can show the class the difference between **sollicitus** and **perterritus**?

Or summarize the events of a story by calling for key words from the story in Latin and writing them on the board. Basic words can be tested simply:

What does **scrībit** mean? What is a **nāvis**?

3 Ask students to suggest Latin words on a specific topic, e.g. "Ten words on the forum before the bell goes—any offers?" or "Ten pairs of opposites, e.g. **puer/puella**." This activity is a useful "filler" and all can contribute.

4 Make flashcards for a fast-paced review requiring only minutes.

5 Because it is easier to remember the meaning of words in context, encourage students to review by rereading the stories themselves.

6 Discuss Latin derivatives in English, Spanish, French, or Italian.

Language information. The explanations and exercises in this section are best used for review and consolidation after students have had considerable experience of all aspects of a feature, e.g. all functions of the dative case. They are not suitable for work on language features which have only recently been introduced. From Stage 8 onwards, teachers will find the charts and exercises helpful in planning additional language practice. Detailed suggestions are made in the Stage commentaries.

The cultural context material

1 Teachers need to vary their treatment of the material, according to the contribution it makes to each Stage. It can be used to:

a) Introduce a Stage or a story, where the content may need to be explored in advance, e.g. Stage 9 (before **in palaestrā** or **in apodytēriō**).

b) Follow up the Latin stories, where it extends the content of the stories, e.g. Stages 3, 6, and 10.

c) Accompany the stories, to help students visualize more clearly the setting for the scenes they are reading, e.g. Stages 4 and 11.

The simplest and most convenient approach, although by no means the only one, is to ask the class to study the material for homework; then the next lesson can begin with an oral (or written) review of the homework, which will lead naturally to class discussion and further questions.

Even where time is short, some class discussion of the cultural features is important. By listening to the different perceptions of their peers, and by testing their own observations in debate, students are helped to extend their powers of observation and their appreciation of different points of view, and learn to develop judgments based on a wider understanding.

In classes where there is a spread of ability, the work given to students will need to be differentiated. For the ablest, the material should provide the introduction to more comprehensive resources in the class or school library; those for whom reading is difficult will need to have their work tailored to a few key paragraphs.

2 The illustrations enable students to envisage the Roman setting and to discover for themselves by observation and deduction more information about the Roman world. In the Stage commentaries teachers have been given additional information to assist their interpretation of the pictures. This should be transmitted to the students only if it seems necessary to aid their understanding and appreciation. Illustrations can be used in a variety of ways:

a) Individual photographs can help students set the scene accurately for a story to be read or acted, e.g. the basilica (p. 46) for the story on p. 44.

b) A group of pictures can be used as the basis for finding out the answers to a set of questions, possibly as a preliminary to reading the cultural context material.

c) Students could be asked to enact what would take place in locations illustrated, e.g. in Stages 8 or 9.

d) The picture essays (e.g. "Streets of Pompeii," pp. 36–37, or "The terrible mountain," p. 173) can form the basis for independent work by students.

3 Encourage students to compile for later reference a portfolio of the materials they collect or produce themselves. They might select topics periodically for more thorough personal study. It is better for students to study a few topics in depth, rather than to attempt to cover everything.

The independent study need not be restricted to written work. Art work, audio or video recording, drama, and modelmaking are all effective ways of exploring and expressing knowledge. Even when time is short, students enjoy being given the opportunity of developing a theme on their own, and it is a good way of encouraging independent learning.

Assessing students' progress

Informal assessment by the teacher is a continuous part of classroom management and lesson planning. It is also essential that formally assessed work be regularly given in class or for homework to provide evidence of individual students' understanding and retention. Students should be fully aware of the criteria for assessment.

There are various assessment tools available with this Course.

- Stage tests focus on the content of each specific Stage and are available to teachers via the *Cambridge Latin Course* website.

- This manual contains diagnostic tests (see Appendix A) to be used after every four Stages to assess the level of student understanding.

- Graded Test booklets are available from CSCP to assess progress at the end of Stages 12, 16, 20, and 28. These booklets include detailed guidance for administering and grading the exams.

Assessment, whether on a final exam or over smaller amounts of material, should emphasize the comprehension of a continuous Latin passage.

Correlation of Unit 1 with the National Latin Exam

Many American and Canadian high-school students take the Level I National Latin Exam (sponsored by the American Classical League and the National Junior Classical League) in early March of their Latin I school year.

Since Latin I students using the Course will normally have reached the middle of Unit 2 by March (*c.* Stage 18), they will be quite prepared to succeed on the Level I exam.

For further information about the National Latin Exam, back copies, and a syllabus, email nle@umw.edu or write to National Latin Exam, University of Mary Washington, 1301 College Avenue, Fredericksburg, VA 22401.

Lesson planning

There are four key principles in lesson planning, whether you are planning a whole Stage, a series of lessons, or a single period.

Motivation. Lessons should have built-in pace and provide regular experience of success for the students. A sense of progress and achievement is the single most motivating factor for students.

Developing independence. A teacher promotes independent reading by having students work individually or in groups for short periods, and by encouraging them to seek help as required.

Integration. The reading materials are not only a medium for acquiring language but also the basis for exploring plot, character, and the Roman world in which the narrative is set. This coherence should constantly be reflected in the work planned for the class.

Variety. Although reading forms the major part of each lesson, the activities pursued by the students, or the work they are set to produce, should be varied to ensure that the lesson has several different phases and momentum is sustained.

An example of a series of three 40-minute lessons is outlined below. It emphasizes some of the typical routines which are the basis of most lessons and also indicates how the pace and detail of each lesson will vary according to the difficulty or subject matter of the material. The series starts at the end of a Stage so that transition to the following Stage can be demonstrated. The timings given for activities are approximate.

1st Period

1 Written test on Vocabulary checklist of a previous Stage; tests handed in (5 mins).
2 Dramatized readings prepared last time (15 mins).
3 Introduction to next Stage: study of opening picture to identify theme (5 mins).
4 Model sentences for next Stage (15 mins):
   (a) Teacher reads pair of sentences.
   (b) Students translate, with help until correct, using line drawings as clues and supported by comprehension questions (in English) from teacher as necessary.
   (c) Repeat with students reading and translating.

2nd Period

1 Teacher comments on test of Vocabulary checklist and returns papers (5 mins).
2 Review of two to three model sentences from last time (5 mins).
3 Comprehension exercise on easy new reading passage (15 mins).
4 Divide next two stories among groups for independent preparation so that each group can tell their story to the rest of the class. Check that each group knows the run-up to their own starting point. Put directions on board to save time (15 mins).

3rd Period

1 Allow time for extra explanation or groups to finish stories (10 mins).
2 Groups tell stories. Students read some extracts aloud in Latin. They are asked to comment on relevant illustrations (20 mins).
3 Teacher picks out and discusses examples of the new language feature as preparation for studying the language note next time (10 mins).
4 Homework: a translation exercise in neat.

Stage commentaries

These notes contain suggestions for planning and teaching Stages 1–12. Each Stage is prefaced by a summary of the content, which is followed by teaching notes for each section in the Stage.

Stories that may be omitted (see p. 10 of this manual) are marked **.

Teachers should feel free to adapt the advice given in the notes to suit their circumstances, either by using suggestions made in the Introduction or by substituting their own ideas.

For further reading on the cultural context material and visual resources consult the Bibliography (pp. 99–101).

STAGE 1: Caecilius

Cultural context
Pompeii; Caecilius and Metella's household;
houses in Pompeii.

Story line
Caecilius and his household are introduced
as they go about their daily business. The dog
tries to steal some food while the cook dozes
in the kitchen.

Main language features
The order in which information is delivered
in a Latin sentence:
- Word order in sentences with **est**.
- Word order in sentences without **est**.

Sentence patterns
NOM + **est** + predicate (N/ADJ)
e.g. *Caecilius est pater.*
NOM + **est** + adverbial prepositional phrase
e.g. *Caecilius est in tablīnō.*
NOM + adverbial prepositional phrase + V
e.g. *pater in tablīnō scrībit.*

Focus of exercises
1   Selection of suitable nominative to
complete sentences with **est**.
2   Selection of suitable prepositional phrase
to complete sentences with and without
est.

Introduction

Ask the class to look at the picture on the front cover. Explain that this is a portrait of a real Roman, Caecilius. Encourage them to speculate how we know about him. Find out what students know about Pompeii. Encourage them to study the portrait, identifying the features that make up the physiognomy (hooked nose, wrinkled forehead, receding hair, expressive eyes, wart), and speculating on the kind of person he might have been. Confirm that in Unit 1 they will be reading about his life and that of his household in Pompeii.

Illustrations: front cover and opening page (p. 1)

Close-up of a bronze portrait head found in the house of Lucius Caecilius Iucundus, Pompeii. The whole head appears on p. 9. The marble shaft supporting the head had the following inscription: **Genio L(uci) nostri Felix l(ibertus)** – *To the guardian spirit of our Lucius, Felix, a freedman, (set this up).*

It has long been considered to be a likeness of Lucius Caecilius Iucundus, the businessman who is the central figure in this book and who occupied the house at the time of the eruption of Vesuvius. Some scholars, however, believe that the head portrays an earlier member of his family, perhaps his father. Nevertheless, it is a clue to our Caecilius' appearance, and the line drawings in this book aim to show a family likeness to this shrewd but kindly face. The head portrayed here is a copy of the original. (We have also introduced a freedman, Felix, in the stories of Stage 6.)

The background on p. 1 is a typical piece of Pompeian wall decoration, a red panel edged with a yellow border reminiscent of embroidery (*Naples, Archaeological Museum*).

Model sentences (pp. 2–5)

New language features. Two basic Latin sentence patterns, one the descriptive statement with **est** (e.g. **Caecilius est pater**), the other the sentence with the verb of action at the end (e.g. **pater in tablīnō scrībit**).

First reading. The line drawings are intended to give the students strong clues so that they can work out for themselves the meaning of the Latin sentences. It is very important to establish the sentence as the basic unit and not to attempt to break it down by analysis at this stage. Note that on pp. 2 and 3 the same sentence pattern is used throughout. On p. 4 that initial pattern is then slightly extended and locates each character in a particular place in the house. Finally, p. 5 builds the sentence pattern further by presenting the character in the same place, and now doing something. The vocabulary is recycled and from the outset the students should be encouraged to read Latin from left to right.

Guide the class through the initial exploration of the model sentences. Read aloud the first sentence or set of sentences in Latin; give students a few moments to make their own attempts to understand. Do not comment about the grammar in advance. Let the students discover the sense of the sentence for themselves, helped by both the narrative and the visual context which generally give strong clues. Most students will grasp the grammatical point of a set of model sentences by the first or second example.

pp. 2–3 Read all the sentences in Latin and invite suggestions from the class about their meaning. Reread and ask for a translation of each.

p. 4 Ask leading questions about the drawings to help the students identify the characters and locations, with the order of your questions reflecting the order of the information in the Latin sentence; e.g.:

Who is in picture 8?

Look at what he is doing. Where do you think he would do that?

Who can now translate the Latin sentence **Caecilius est in tablīnō**?

In looking at the pictures for clues, students will ask questions and make observations about the rooms. Accept these, but keep comment brief so that attention is focused on the Latin sentences. After exploring the sentences with the class, ask individuals to read a sentence in Latin and translate it. Handle prepositional phrases such as **in ātriō** as a single unit, and encourage students to supply the definite or indefinite article in English as appropriate.

p. 5 This page points up the differing word order of sentences with **est** and those with other verbs. The formula "find the subject, find the verb" is not appropriate and, if used, will become increasingly problematic as the sentence structures develop throughout the Course. Instead, as on pp. 2–4, encourage students to read the Latin left to right, so that from the outset they become used to receiving information in the order in which it flows in Latin.

Give students a few moments to look at each picture and the accompanying Latin sentences. Then ask questions in English, using the picture as a guide. The technique of asking questions in this situation requires much thought and care. Couch the questions in concrete terms. For example:

fīlia in hortō legit.
Q. Who is in the picture?
A. The daughter.
Q. Good. Where is she?
A. In the garden.
Q. Good. Is she writing or walking or reading?

A. Reading.

Q. Excellent. So what does the whole sentence mean?

A. The daughter is in the garden reading.

Q. Very good. How else might we say that in English?

A. The daughter is reading in the garden.

Students may make comments or ask questions. If so, confirm correct observations and help the students to form their own conclusions about what they observe. Do not yourself initiate discussion about the language until they have read the story which follows and are ready for About the language (p. 7).

Students may translate **servus in cubiculō labōrat** (and similar sentences) as *The slave is in the bedroom working*. Do not reject this version but encourage alternatives, and students will themselves arrive at *The slave is working in the bedroom* or *The slave works in the bedroom*.

After this, discuss the line drawings more fully and follow up with work on the cultural context material (pp. 8–13). Among the points to note in the line drawings are:

1   Caecilius' **familia** included his slaves and freedmen and freedwomen, as well as his wife and children (the number of slaves shown in the picture is an estimate; guesses at how many slaves might have lived in and around Caecilius' house vary wildly depending on how much or how little sleeping space was allotted to them); Caecilius' slightly grubby toga: it would have been impossible to keep the toga pristine; colored clothing: the Romans were not clad in white all the time.

2   Metella's chalk-white skin, achieved using cosmetics. It is not known which women wore this very pale makeup, nor how much of the time or how extensively over their exposed skin, but we have imagined Metella to favor a very pale look.

7   Cerberus named after the mythical guard dog of Hades.

8   The study opening onto the garden; writing with pen and ink on a papyrus scroll; lamp standard (front right) with container for scrolls behind.

9   The atrium as seen from the study; front door at far end with shrine to **larēs** at left; aperture in roof to admit air, light, and water, with pool to collect rainwater below; little furniture.

10 Small dining table, with couches for reclining at dinner.

11 Courtyard garden with colonnade for shelter from sun, plants in tubs and beds, statues, and fountain to refresh the air.

12 Bedroom with little furniture besides a couch, cupboard, and small table.

13 Cooking pots on charcoal fires, fuel store underneath.

14 Chained guard dog at front door; high curb; no front lawn.

15 Oil lamp on stand; wax tablets and **stilus** (contrast with 8 above).

21 The door open, but guarded, to allow air to flow through into the house and enable passersby to view the wealth of the owner.

General   It has long been known that some (although not all) of the "red" discovered by archaeologists on the walls of Pompeii was in fact not red lead and cinnabar, but rather yellow ochre which was turned red by the hot gases from the eruption of Vesuvius. Italy's National Institute of Optics has suggested that the balance between red and yellow would have been almost 50:50, but other scholars are doubtful that it is possible to be sure about the proportion of red to yellow. In the face of such doubt, the line drawings of Caecilius' house use a substantial amount of Pompeian red, on the assumption that Caecilius would have been able to afford the expensive red pigment for his walls. Yellow also has a significant presence, to remind users that we should not exaggerate the dominance of Pompeian red on the walls of the city.

Consolidation. Students could reread the model sentences for homework. At the beginning of the next lesson, give the students a few minutes in pairs to review the model sentences and refresh their memories, and then ask individuals to read and translate a sentence.

In subsequent lessons, use single sentences as a quick oral drill, and then gradually modify them, e.g. **Caecilius in tablīnō labōrat** (instead of **scrībit**).

Cerberus (p. 6)

Story. Whilst everyone is occupied, Cerberus the dog jumps onto the kitchen table in search of food. Startled by a snore from the sleeping Grumio, he barks and is discovered.

First reading. The story divides naturally into two parts: the household going about its daily business and the scene in the kitchen. Take each paragraph separately as follows:

1   Read it in Latin, clearly and expressively. For example, illustrate the growling sound by vigorously rolling the "r"s of **Cerberus** and **lātrat**.
2   Give students time to explore the meaning in pairs or groups.
3   Reread the passage in Latin.
4   Invite suggestions for the meaning. Then develop a translation in groups or as a class.

For more senior students, a dramatic reading by the teacher of the entire second paragraph, slowly enough for students to glance at the new vocabulary alongside, is often enough to lead students to comprehension of the story line.

Consolidation. Encourage students to comment on the characters, and allow them to respond to the story in different ways; interest in character and situation is a very important factor in developing reading skill.

Other possible consolidation strategies for younger students might include:

1   Cartoons by the students or the teacher.
2   Miming of the story by students. Label sections of the classroom to correspond with the rooms in the story. Read the story aloud while the students mime the actions. Props optional.

Illustration. Mosaic inside the entrance to Caecilius' house. It was common in well-to-do Pompeian houses to have a black-and-white mosaic picture just inside the door, which normally stood open in the daytime. Often this showed a watchdog. Compare Caecilius' relaxed animal with the **cavē canem** mosaic, p. 179. What does the depiction of the dog suggest about the character of the master of the family who commissioned such a mosaic?

About the language (p. 7)

New language feature. The different word order in Latin sentences according to whether the verb is **est** or not.

Discussion. The focus here is the sentence as a whole; avoid breaking it down into parts. Take paragraphs 1 and 2 together as the core of the note, and paragraph 3 on its own.

Encourage students to read Latin from left to right from the outset, and to become used to information flowing in a different order from English.

Consolidation. Ask the students to find similar examples in the model sentences or the story.

Practicing the language (p. 7)

Exercise 1. Practice in the structure of sentences with **est**.

Exercise 2. Completion of sentence with appropriate prepositional phrase.

Note. These two exercises aim to consolidate students' knowledge of the characters as well as the language. All options may be possible, but encourage students to select options which make good sense (usually based on the stories or model sentences) and to avoid answers which, though structurally feasible, produce unlikely situations. Writing out correctly a complete Latin sentence and its translation, however easy, reinforces students' confidence and grasp of the language. In Stage 1 it may be useful for the teacher to guide students, as they write answers in their notebooks for the first time, by doing one or two sentences, or even all of exercise 1 together before assigning the rest of the work in class or as homework.

Cultural context material (pp. 8–13)

Content. Students are introduced to the members of the household and the house in which they lived and worked.

Suggestions for discussion. The material can be taken in two parts, starting with the sections on Caecilius and Metella. Students could be asked to read this for homework after they have met members of the household in the model sentences. The following class discussion might include:

1 What qualities Caecilius, as a successful businessman, would look for in his wife.
2 The position of women in Roman society compared to our own.

Following a reading of the notes on housing, discussions could include:

3 The contrast between modern houses and the Pompeian **domus urbāna**. Beside the differences in layout, discuss reasons for the more inward-looking orientation of the Pompeian house. Consider also the means of running it: slaves, water supply, toilets and bathing facilities, types of fuel, and appliances for heating and lighting.
4 The effects of slaves on a household.
5 How we can reconstruct Pompeian houses and gardens on the basis of archaeological findings.

Further information. The figure of 10,000 for the total population of Pompeii can only be approximate. According to Beard, current estimates vary from 6,400 to 30,000. See Beard for further details.

Caecilius The basis of our knowledge about Caecilius is 153 wax tablets containing his business records, which were discovered in 1875 in a strongbox or **arca**, in his house. The tablets indicate the range and diversity of Caecilius' financial interests. They include records of a loan, sales of timber and land, the rent for a laundry and for land leased from the town council, and the auction of linen on behalf of an Egyptian merchant. His commission was 2 percent.

A graffito found in the house says: *He who loves should live; he who knows not how to love should die; and he who obstructs love should die twice.* A wine amphora found in the shop at the right of the housefront reads: **Caecilio Iucundo ab Sexsto Metello** (*To Caecilius Iucundus from Sextus Metellus*). An election notice mentions Caecilius' two sons: **Ceium Secundum IIvirum Quintus et Sextus Caecili Iucundi rogant** (*Quintus Caecilius and Sextus Caecilius ask for Ceius Secundus as duovir*). This inscription gives us Quintus as the **praenōmen** (personal name) of the son. For simplicity in our stories, we have omitted mention of Sextus. The names attributed to the rest of the household are invented. Lucia, Caecilius' fictional daughter, is not—as she should be—called Caecilia (too confusing), but instead has acquired her name from her father's praenomen.

Visible from the street are the mosaic of the dog on p. 6 and the view shown on p. 12. The contents of the house (including several wall paintings) are currently in storage either in Pompeii or in the Archaeological Museum in Naples. Unfortunately, the famous marble lararium relief (illustration pp. 52, 166–167), depicting scenes from the disastrous earthquake of AD 62 or 63, has been stolen and is accessible only in photographs.

Metella On p. 5 Metella is shown seated in the atrium so that she could oversee the work of the household slaves. This would have formed an important part of her daily duties.

By the time of our stories the old forms of marriage had given way to a freer form in which the wife could, with little trouble, end an unsuitable marriage by divorce while retaining possession of her own property, subject only to supervision by a guardian. Such guardianship was, apparently, treated merely as a formality and a woman had only to apply for a change in guardian if she found him unsuitable. After the time of Augustus (63 BC – AD 14), a woman could inherit property, although the law restricted the amount. Women found ingenious ways of circumventing this law: several were themselves full heirs and passed on their property to chosen heirs through their wills.

Most of our knowledge about the status of women refers to those in the upper class. A Roman girl's life would vary according to her social status. A daughter in the upper class would not work outside the home, but would be instructed by her mother and would help her mother in supervising the household. She would have the freedom, unheard of in ancient Athens, to visit her friends, go to the baths, and shop. The daughters in lower-class families might be expected to work in the family business. In addition to the wide range of occupations women were known to engage in, students are intrigued to learn that some women even became gladiators.

When a Roman matron went out, her **stola mātrōnālis** won her recognition, prestige, and respect. She was expected to have management skills and exerted a responsible and independent influence in the household. She often managed her own property outside the household as well. The students may be interested to learn that Varro's first book on farming was dedicated to his wife and was intended to guide her in managing her own land. There were so many women with shipbuilding interests that the Emperor Claudius offered them special rewards if they cooperated in his new harbor and shipbuilding program.

Students often ask about the naming of girls and women. Originally a Roman woman had only one name, usually the feminine form of her father's **nōmen**. Gaius Julius Caesar's daughter was called Julia. If there were more than one daughter, the names would be the same, distinguished by words such as "the elder," "the younger," "the first," "the second," "the third": Julia Maior or Julia Prima, Julia Minor or Julia Secunda. A woman retained her name after marriage. By the time of our stories, two names had bec common, the first the woman's family name, the second taken from her father, her mother, or another family member.

Houses in Pompeii The ground plan of a Pompeian house, as printed in the textbook, p. 11, has been simplified to show the basic components of the **domus urbāna**. In reality, the house of Caecilius was more elaborate than the house depicted. In fact, his house and the one to the north had been renovated to become a single house. Once students have become familiar with the layout of a simple urban house, they may go on to study, interpret, or copy the plans of actual Pompeian houses.

You might wish to elaborate on the function of the atrium. This was the formal or ceremonial center of the house. Here the marriage couch was placed for the wedding night, here the patron received his clients, here the young man donned the **toga virīlis**, and here the body lay in state on a funeral couch.

Illustrations

p. 8
- The front of Caecilius' house on the Via Vesuvio, which is the northern part of Stabiae Street (plan, p. 34). Like many prosperous houses, it has, on each side of the tall, imposing front door, shops which might have been leased out or managed by the owner's slaves or freedmen. The adjoining house further up the street also belonged to Caecilius; part of the common wall had been renovated to permit access between the houses.
- Caecilius leased a laundry from the town council, but we do not know where it was. The one illustrated is the laundry of Stephanus in the Via dell' Abbondanza. We see a large tank for washing cloth in the front of the shop. More were installed in the yard at the back, and drying and bleaching (using urine) were carried out on the flat roof. A tunic cost 1 denarius to launder.
- Map of the Bay of Naples.

p. 9
- The bronze head from Caecilius' house (see Introduction p. 21).
- One of the carbonized tablets from Caecilius' archives, with a drawing of another showing the writing.
- Wood and bronze strongbox similar to the one in which Caecilius kept his tablets (*Naples, Archaeological Museum*).
- A bronze sestertius, a silver denarius, and a gold aureus.

p. 10
- Hairstyle from the Flavian period. Juvenal (*Satire* 6.502–504) jokes about the construction of this hairstyle, and the way in which it makes the woman look much taller from the front than from behind (*Rome, Capitoline Museums*).

p. 11
- Diagram showing the typical features of the Roman atrium house. These houses are common in Pompeii, though with many individual variations; there are also smaller houses and apartments.
- Facade of the House of the Wooden Partition, Herculaneum, chosen in preference to one at Pompeii because of its more complete preservation. The doors open directly onto the sidewalk and the windows are small and high up. The house is faced with painted stucco. The house further down the street, built over the sidewalk, is timber-framed and contains a number of separate apartments.

p. 12 • The atrium of the House of Menander (named after the painting of the playwright found in the house), one of the grandest houses in Pompeii. The vista in the photograph was contrived to impress visitors and passersby who would be able to see through the open front door. In the atrium we can see the **compluvium**, with the **impluvium** below. Behind, two columns frame the **tablīnum** with the **peristȳlium** beyond; a corridor to the left allowed access to the garden at times when the master desired privacy in the **tablīnum**, which could be closed off by a curtain. In the far distance are some of the rooms opening off the peristyle. These offered more privacy for the family than the more formal and public atrium.

• Atrium of Caecilius' house, showing the **impluvium**, the mosaic floor, and a little surviving painted plaster on the walls. We also see (from the left) the space called an **āla** (wing) that often opens off an atrium, the doorway of the hall providing access to the garden, the **tablīnum**, and garden behind. To the left of the **tablīnum** is the pedestal which supported the bronze head (cf. pp. 1, 9).

• A **larārium**. Statuettes of the **larēs** (protective spirits of the family, cf. p. 167) and offerings of food, wine, and flowers would have been placed in this little shrine; its back wall might have been decorated with pictures of the household gods (lares and penates) and, often, protective snakes.

p. 13 • Caecilius' tablinum. It had a rather plain mosaic floor and painted walls, with pictures of nymphs and satyrs on white rectangles against colored panels designed to suggest hanging tapestries.

• Wall painting from the House of Venus in the Shell, Pompeii. The walls of gardens were often painted with trees, flowers, trellises, birds, and fountains to supplement the real garden and give the illusion that it was larger.

• A small but well-preserved peristyle in the House of the Relief of Telephus, Herculaneum. Decorative carved marble disks hang between the columns. Garlands of flowers and foliage would be draped between these and the columns on festive occasions.

p. 14 Examples of Roman jewelry of the period: a gold snake bracelet and a snake ring cast solid and finely chased; a pair of emerald cluster earrings; and one of a pair of hollow gold ball earrings (*London, British Museum*).

Suggestions for further activities

1 Research a named Roman woman (e.g. Agrippina; Seneca's mother, Helvia; Cicero's daughter, Tullia; Cicero's wife, Terentia; Augustus' wife, Livia; etc.) and prepare a short biography.

2 Research and compare the status of women in the Greek world with that of women in the Roman world.

3 Research the meaning of your name. With the help of a dictionary and your teacher, make a **bulla** on which you put your first name Latinized (**praenōmen**), your family name translated as closely as possible in Latin (**nōmen**), and a chosen Latin nickname (**cognōmen**). For example, Thomas Cook who plays the bagpipes: Tomaso Coquus Tibicen.

4   Using a picture from Stage 1 as a centerpiece, write a real estate agent's advertisement for a Pompeian house, describing its amenities.

Vocabulary checklist (p. 14)

Students will already be familiar with all or most of these words, since they will have occurred several times in the material. It is helpful to ask them to recall the context in which they met a word because the association will often fix it in their minds. Discussion of derivations is valuable for extending students' vocabulary in English and other modern languages and will also reinforce their grasp of Latin.

STAGE 2: in vīllā

<table>
<tr><td>

Cultural context
Pompeian daily life; clothing; food.

Story line
Dinner party. Grumio enjoys himself as
Caecilius and his guest sleep off their meal.

Main language features
- Nominative and accusative singular.

</td><td>

Sentence patterns
NOM + ACC + V
e.g. *amīcus Caecilium salūtat.*
NOM + ACC + V et V
e.g. *Grumiō triclīnium intrat et circumspectat.*

Focus of exercises
1 Completion of sentence with suitable
   noun, verb, or phrase.
2 Completion of sentence with suitable
   verb.
3 Story for translation.

</td></tr>
</table>

Opening page (p. 15)

Illustration. Reconstructed bedroom from a villa at Boscoreale, near Pompeii, owned by
Publius Fannius Synistor, a very wealthy man. The high elegant bed (or it may in fact be a
dining couch) with its pillow bolsters requires an equally elegant stepping stool. The walls
are decorated with architectural panels drawn from theater scenes of comedy, tragedy, and
satyr plays (*New York, Metropolitan Museum of Art*).

Model sentences (pp. 16–19)

New language feature. The accusative is introduced not in isolation but in the context of
a common sentence pattern: NOM + ACC + V.

New vocabulary. amīcus, salūtat, spectat, parātus, gustat, anxius, laudat, vocat.

First reading. Introduce the situation briefly, e.g. "A friend (**amīcus**) is visiting Caecilius."
Then take the first pair of sentences as follows: *Sentence 1.* Read in Latin, then ask who
is in the picture and where he is. *Sentence 2.* Read in Latin, then explore the situation,
e.g. "Who is in the picture with Caecilius? What is he doing?" Read the Latin sentence
again and ask for the meaning. Encourage a variety of meanings for **salūtat**, e.g. *says hello,
greets.* The main aim is to establish the correct grammatical relationship between **amīcus**
and **Caecilium**. If students ask, "Isn't his name Caecilius?", congratulate the students for
noticing the change and confirm that they should continue to use the form Caecilius. Do
not enter into explanations yet, but encourage students to look for patterns as you read the
following sentences.

Repeat the process with each pair of sentences as far as 10. Most students are quick to
understand the new sentence pattern.

Run through sentences 1–10 quickly again, with pairs of students for each pair of
sentences. Students should read their sentences aloud and translate them.

Then follow the same process with the picture story about Metella in sentences 11–20.

If there are questions about the new endings, ask the students if they can suggest what
the new endings indicate. This is not the time to introduce the terminology of "nominative"

and "accusative," but it is the time to encourage the students first to look for patterns and then propose some theories about those patterns. Suggest they test their theories in the reading that follows. Be flexible, however, if you feel that students already understand the point.

Consolidation. Reuse the pairs of sentences for quick oral drill in the next lesson or two, to reinforce the natural English word order for translating the second sentence.

mercātor (p. 20)

Story. Caecilius is working in the study when a merchant calls for dinner. Grumio keeps them waiting.

First reading. This simple story comes to life for the class if first read aloud in Latin by the teacher with good phrasing (to help the students understand which words group together), dramatic interpretation, and well-controlled pace. It is important to:

1 Teach the class to look at new words in their context first, consulting the vocabulary list only when necessary.
2 Ask leading questions to elicit the meaning of a paragraph or group of sentences, and encourage a range of different interpretations before agreeing on a formal version.
3 Follow up hints at character and attitude (e.g. Grumio's cheerful and extroverted nature, Caecilius' irritation) and information about the daily work of Caecilius and Grumio.

As an alternative, this story and the next lend themselves to an illustrative approach, using your own artwork or artwork provided by the students.

Consolidation. The class should acquire a sound grasp of the story, language, and cultural content. Rereading should be as varied as possible and might include activities like:

1 A group attempt to achieve the closest and most natural English version.
2 A reenactment of the story.
3 Isolating some of the sentences containing the accusative and asking for their meaning.
4 Inviting speculation about what will follow the end of the story.

Refer students to the description of Caecilius' business interests (p. 8) and the "Daily life" note (pp. 23–24), including the picture of bankers (p. 23). For illustrations relating to Grumio's work see the model sentences on pp. 18–19 and pp. 21, 25, and 26.

in triclīniō (p. 20)

Story. The dinner served by Grumio is a success, as is the after-dinner entertainment. When Caecilius and his guest take a nap, Grumio makes himself at home.

First reading. The students will be able to visualize this story if it is linked with the information about meals and Roman food (pp. 24–25), which could be read for homework in advance.

This story is best handled in sections. Encourage students to develop the habit of using the context to establish the sense of a passage, returning later to clarify details.

Consolidation. Use various ways of rereading the text (see the Introduction, pp. 13–14). Ask the class to comment on Caecilius' praise of Grumio after his earlier reprimand, and on Grumio's opportunistic behavior.

About the language (p. 21)

New language feature. The difference in function and form between the nominative and accusative. Discussion of declensions is postponed until Stage 3.

Discussion. Start by putting one pair of model sentences on the board (e.g. **Caecilius est in ātriō. amīcus Caecilium salūtat.**)

> Q: **Caecilius** appears in both sentences, but there is a difference between the ways in which he appears in the Latin. Point out the difference.
> A: In one he is **Caecilius**, in the other **Caecilium**.
> Q: Good. Both these Latin words mean "Caecilius," but they have different forms. Suggest an explanation for this.

Guide the students to realize that **Caecilius** is used when he *does* the action and **Caecilium** when he *receives* the action. Then put up other sentences with accusatives (including endings in -**am**, -**um**, -**em**) and invite comment. As students grasp the grammatical pattern, introduce them to the names (nominative and accusative) for the two different forms of the noun. Student observations will usually include:

1 The nominative (subject) shows someone who does something.
2 The accusative (object) shows someone who has something done to him or her.
3 The accusative ends in -**m**.
4 The Latin accusative follows the nominative, but the English translation has the corresponding word at the end.

Then study About the language. Add further examples if necessary, always in complete sentences, using familiar words and retaining the nominative + accusative + verb word order. Concentrate on using the terms "nominative" and "accusative" and their characteristic endings, rather than introducing additional terms such as "subject" and "object." If students themselves use these terms, confirm that they are correct, but continue to use the case names.

Consolidation. Go back to the stories on p. 20 and ask students to pick out nominatives and accusatives. For instance, taking **in triclīniō**: "What case is **coquum** in line 6? How do you know? In **coquus ancillam spectat** (line 13), which word is nominative? How can you tell?" Sometimes ask for the translation of the sentence under discussion, to remind students of the grammatical relationship shown by the case names.

Illustration. Peacock wall painting (*Naples, Archaeological Museum*).

Practicing the language (p. 22)

Exercise 1. Practice in the structure of a simple sentence. Students use the sense and structure of the sentence to insert the missing item (noun, verb, or prepositional phrase).

Exercise 2. Completion of sentence with a verb, selected according to sense. Incidental reinforcement of the accusative. In sentence **i**, **cēnam** and **canem** may cause confusion. The English derivative *canine* may help.

Exercise 3. Story. A friend visits Grumio and helps himself to food before Grumio appears. The exercise provides a good opportunity to review two details about translation from Stage 1. Introduce a discussion of English idiom by comparing translations of the following sentences:

>**amīcus Grumiōnem vīsitat. amīcus est servus.**
>
>1 The friend visits Grumio. The friend is a slave.
>2 The friend is visiting Grumio. The friend is a slave.
>3 A friend is visiting Grumio. The friend is a slave.

Ask students to explain the differences and to discuss which they prefer in the context. The same discussion concerning the translation of the verb could center on the sentence **amīcus cibum cōnsūmit**.

Cultural context material (pp. 23–25)

Content. A brief description of daily life including meals, dress, and the **salūtātiō** (morning visit).

Suggestions for discussion. Material is best introduced where it relates to the stories, e.g. p. 23 with **mercātor** (p. 20), and pp. 24–25 with **in triclīniō** (p. 20).

Further information. Because students are likely to ask many questions about meals and food, you might prepare by consulting Apicius and McLeish for Roman recipes.

Informal family meals including **iēntāculum** (breakfast) and **prandium** (lunch) were eaten standing or sitting; reclining on one's elbow was a formality generally practiced at the **cēna** (dinner), especially when guests were present. After the time of Augustus, it became common practice for the women also to recline (instead of sitting on chairs beside the couches).

The times of meals and work during the Roman day were earlier than ours. This information could provoke discussion of the effect of the Mediterranean climate on daily life then and now and of the absence of strong artificial light in the ancient world. The use of sundials (see illustration on p. 137) might raise questions about how accurately and how often the Romans needed to tell the time. The Romans divided the daylight time into twelve hours. The sundial picture can be used to elicit the point that an hour (i.e. one-twelfth of the period of daylight) could be forty-five minutes in midwinter, seventy-five in midsummer.

At a dinner party the guest of honor would be placed at the **locus cōnsulāris (locus īmus)** on the **lectus medius**, where he would be beside the host and host's family on the **lectus īmus**.

Peacocks (illustrations, pp. 19, 21) were popular in the Roman world not only as food and wall decorations, but also as live ornaments in gardens.

Illustrations

p. 23   ● Roman dressed in toga. Honorific marble statue from Herculaneum (*Naples, Archaeological Museum*).

       ● Relief, *c.* AD 230, showing two bankers, the one on the left with a scroll and the one on the right with a money bag. Someone is bringing them a bag of money on his shoulder. The counter has a protective barrier at the right side (*Rome, Museo Nazionale Romano*).

p. 24 ● Plan of a **triclīnium**.
　　　● Carbonized loaf of bread found in Pompeii (*Naples, Archaeological Museum*).
p. 25 ● Bowl of eggs found in Pompeii (*Naples, Archaeological Museum*).
　　　● A popular subject for a triclinium floor was food, particularly fish. Detail from a larger mosaic depicting a fight between an octopus and a lobster, from a triclinium in the House of the Faun, Pompeii. This mosaic shows different species of seafood, including here a small spotted cat shark (left), sea bass (right), and red mullet (bottom right). Pompeii had a lively fish trade and produced and exported fish sauces (**garum**). Many jars have been found in distant sites bearing the label of a prosperous Pompeii packager, Umbricius Scaurus, whose tomb is shown on p. 95 (*Naples, Archaeological Museum*).
　　　● Wall painting of a larder (*Naples, Archaeological Museum*).
　　　● Bowl of fruit in the villa of the Poppaei family at Oplontis. Note the artist's skill in showing transparent glass.
　　　● Basket of figs in the dining room of the villa at Oplontis.
p. 26　Bronze cooking pots and trivets on a charcoal hearth in the kitchen of the House of the Vettii, Pompeii.

Suggestions for discussion

1 Reasons why times for Roman meals and work were earlier than ours. Artificial light has facilitated changes in social habits. Students may note that the daily schedule in the Mediterranean is still similar to the Roman one.
2 Methods of telling time.
3 The kinds of decoration that Pompeians often painted on the walls of the triclinium (using illustrations from the textbook or the website).

Suggestions for further activities

1 As a baker and a **cliēns** of Caecilius, write an account of your morning visit to Caecilius' house. Include a description of your surroundings and the conversations that occur.
2 Design an invitation to a Roman dinner party, with the menu and a description of the entertainments.
3 Sample some Roman dishes or simulate a Roman dinner party. Stuffed dates, ham and figs, and pork and apricots are easy. Pickled eggs, alcohol-free wine, olives, grapes, and almonds can be bought from any supermarket.
4 Look at the examples of wall paintings in the first four Stages. Then design a simple wall panel and color appropriately.
5 Make an illustrated diary of a day in the life of Caecilius and the same for Metella. Set them side by side so that they can be compared.

STAGE 3: negōtium

Cultural context
Pompeian town life and business.

Story line
Caecilius goes to work in the forum. Clara paints a mural in Caecilius' house. Caecilius visits Pantagathus, a barber. He buys a slave girl from Syphax, the slave dealer.

Main language features
- Nominative and accusative of 1st, 2nd, and 3rd declensions.

Sentence patterns
V + NOM
e.g. *respondet Pantagathus.*

Focus of exercises
1   Selection of suitable verb.
2   Selection of nominative or accusative.

Opening page (p. 27)

Illustration. This wall painting of an unidentified harbor, found at Stabiae (a cluster of villas on the Bay of Naples), introduces the theme of commerce. A dock encloses a harbor where ships stand at anchor. In the foreground are small fishing boats. Visible along the harbor side are (from the left) colonnades with marble ornaments hanging between the columns, docks, rich colonnaded buildings, large merchant ships, commemorative pillars carrying statues of prominent citizens, and a colonnaded street behind which is a series of gabled structures, perhaps warehouses. A small lighthouse stands on a rocky outcropping (*Naples, Archaeological Museum*).

Model sentences

Because this Stage is designed to help students integrate their previous knowledge, it contains no model sentences.

**in forō (p. 28)

(Stories with a double asterisk are those which can be omitted by those moving quickly through the Course. The story line should be summarized for the students. See Introduction, p. 10.)

Story. Caecilius is in the forum, conducting his business as a banker, and meets Clara the wall painter and Pantagathus the barber. Syphax the slave dealer is angry because a merchant misses an appointment.

First reading. Read the story aloud dramatically so that students gain an impression of the range of people and occurrences in the forum. Refer to the line drawing to introduce the characters and their surroundings, and use a series of quick questions to keep the pace of interpretation brisk.

Consolidation. In discussion, establish the forum as the center of social and business life in Pompeii. Draw on the students' knowledge of Caecilius' business interests as an **argentārius** (Stage 1, pp. 8–9). This is a good story for students to practice reading aloud, to develop confidence and accuracy in pronunciation.

Illustration. The line drawing shows the forum as it would have looked before the earthquake of AD 62 or 63: a large paved space, lined on both sides by colonnades with a second floor, a pre-eruption Vesuvius behind. The temple of Jupiter can be seen (center) flanked by arches with honorific statues of the emperor's family. At the time of this story, in AD 79, the forum was still being repaired.

artifex (p. 29)

Story. Clara is welcomed by Quintus and taken by Metella to the dining room, where she paints a mural which meets with Lucia's approval.

First reading. Divide the story into two sections, lines 1–8 and 9–end. After reading the first section aloud in Latin, use comprehension questions with the whole group (cf. pp. 12–13 above). Then translate the second section in pairs initially, referring to the picture, followed by group comments and comparisons.

Language. Students have already met prepositional phrases (**in ātriō, in vīllā**) and this story introduces more (**ad vīllam, ad iānuam, ad triclīnium**). From hearing you reading the Latin, the students should naturally handle these phrases as complete units and not split them into separate words.

Adjectives have so far been used predicatively (**coquus est laetus**) and are now being used attributively (**magnus leō, magnum fūstem**). This should cause students no difficulty in understanding and should not be analyzed until Stages 14 and 18 in Unit 2, where there are notes on adjectives.

Consolidation. Students can easily mime this story while a narrator reads the Latin, or different students reread the sentences concerned with the different characters: artifex, Metella, canis, etc. The student Clara can draw the wall painting on the board.

Further information. Clara represents one of the many women of Pompeii who worked to earn their living as, inter alia, traders and artisans. A list of female artists appears in Pliny the Elder, and there is a wall painting in Pompeii's House of the Surgeon of a female artist at work. Clara's name is borrowed from Verania Clara, a freedwoman whose name appeared in a funerary inscription in Pompeii's Nucerian Gate necropolis. In the absence of any precedent for the use of the term **pictrix**, Clara is described as **artifex**, a term often used to describe painters by Pliny the Elder, and also employed (in a somewhat less positive context) in Tacitus' *Annals* 12 to describe a woman who was an "artist" at administering poison! Clara is typical of Campanian artists of the period who reproduced Greek subjects, often from Greek originals, but who showed skills which made them more than mere copyists. Here Hercules is engaged in the first of his Twelve Labors, overcoming the Nemean lion.

Illustrations. The three small pictures (*Naples, Archaeological Museum*) are chosen to illustrate a range of popular themes. The shepherd boy with pipes has pointed ears because he is a satyr. Cupids are found everywhere engaged in everyday activities ranging from winemaking to chariot racing to catching a rabbit (pictured). The portrait is possibly a poet, holding a rolled-up scroll and wearing a garland.

tōnsor (p. 30)

Story. While Caecilius waits his turn at the barber's, a poet recites a rude rhyme which so infuriates Pantagathus that an accident occurs.

First reading. Read the story aloud in as dramatic a manner as possible and ascertain, by general questioning in English, how much students have understood. Some may have grasped the situation immediately. The word order VERB + NOMINATIVE, e.g. **respondet Pantagathus**, is used here for the first time, but needs no comment.

Comprehension questions. Use these after the whole passage has been read and when you think students are ready to tackle them successfully. The questions are designed to encourage the students to think about the meaning of the passage, rather than simply translating Latin into English. Question 8 requires a quotation from the story in Latin, but the other questions should be answered in English. The aim of the Course is to develop, as rapidly and efficiently as possible, students' ability to read for meaning, rather than to compose Latin.

The website has comprehension questions built into many of the stories from the outset, but this is the first time comprehension questions occur in the student book. They may serve as rough models when you are planning your own questions. When authoring comprehension questions, consider whether the aim of your questions is to help and guide the students through the story, or to assess them on their understanding. Consider, also, asking some questions which address the surface meaning of the Latin (such as Question 1) and some (such as the second part of Question 7) which encourage the students to think beyond the text itself.

Consolidation. If students have managed the comprehension questions well, there is no need for further consolidation. If not, assign part of the story for a written translation.

Further information. Pantagathus has a name suggesting Greek origins. At this time Roman men were generally clean shaven and visited the barber at some time during the morning, so that his shop became the center of news and gossip. In the line drawing he is shown using a folding razor of Roman design. The poet's visit is a reminder that the customary way for writers to draw attention to their work was by reciting or reading it aloud.

vēnālīcius (p. 31)

Story. Caecilius seeks out the slave dealer to buy a new slave and returns home with a pretty slave girl whose arrival provokes mixed reactions.

First reading. Discuss the line drawing and establish that Syphax deals in slaves from overseas. Then explore the story with comprehension questions, e.g.:

1   In the first paragraph find the word which suggests where Syphax has come from.
2   Why, in line 9, does Syphax call for wine? (Some students will see this as a way of softening up Caecilius, others as a chance to introduce Melissa.)
3   In lines 13–14, what are Melissa's skills, according to Syphax? (Some students may translate **Melissa cēnam optimam coquit** (line 13) as *Melissa cooks very good dinners* or *Melissa cooks dinner very well*. Such answers reveal that they have understood the meaning of the text. The class can be guided toward *Melissa cooks a very good dinner* by asking "What kind of dinner does Melissa cook?"

Consolidation. Translation of this story enables the class to discuss the most appropriate English for such phrases as **salvē, Syphāx!** spoken by a businessman; **ancilla Caecilium dēlectat**; and **ēheu!**

The last paragraph of the story usually provokes a lively discussion of the characters and their attitudes. The students should see that Melissa is quite literally the "object" (bought at the market) of Grumio's and Quintus' attention or, possibly, unsolicited affection. Do not, however, allow students to lay facile charges of "male chauvinism." They should attempt to comprehend the familial and psychological problems that slavery, as part of the Roman system, caused.

If students have not asked already, this story may provoke questions about slavery in general. Answer only the questions asked and assure students that they will be investigating the topic more fully in Stage 6. If you yourself are unsure about some particular detail regarding slavery, prepare yourself for such questions by reading the teacher's manual and the cultural context material in the students' textbook for that Stage.

Further information. Syphax, an imaginary character like Clara and Pantagathus, is an astute Syrian who makes his living in the slave trade, bringing skilled as well as manual laborers to the Italian market.

Illustrations. Shears of the kind illustrated were used instead of scissors (*Museum of London*). Troublesome slaves might be shackled to prevent escape (*Cambridge, Museum of Archaeology and Anthropology*).

About the language (p. 32)

New language feature. Nouns are displayed in declensions (nominative and accusative of 1st, 2nd, and 3rd declensions only).

Discussion. Note the forms, and stress that knowledge of one example within a declension is the key to all or most of the others. Encourage the concept that this new term, "declension," is roughly equivalent to a "family."

Consolidation. Follow discussion of the note with more oral review of the nominative and accusative cases:

1   Give students an English sentence and ask them to say which word would be in the nominative/accusative.

2   Using one of the Stage 3 stories, ask students to pick out nominatives and accusatives which they have already met in context. For instance, in **vēnālīcius**: "What case is **servum** in line 6? Which word is nominative in **Caecilius Melissam emit** in line 15?" Some students may be able to recognize which declension each noun belongs to. Occasionally ask for a translation to remind students of the function of the two cases.

3   With p. 32 open, and using only the examples in the tables provided, ask students to give the Latin for a word in an English sentence, e.g.:
        I entered *the shop*.
        The merchant bought *the slave*.

Illustration. Golden oriole (*Naples, Archaeological Museum*).

Practicing the language (p. 33)

Exercise 1. Selection of verb according to sense.

Exercise 2. Selection of nominative or accusative singular.

These exercises should not present any major difficulties. If students have trouble with the phrase **ē vīllā** in the first sentence of exercise 1, refer them back to the parallel phrase, **ē tabernā**, in the story **tōnsor**, p. 30, line 13.

Cultural context material (pp. 33–37)

Content. An overview of the layout of Pompeii, its main features, and its links with the rest of the Roman empire.

Suggestions for discussion. The map of Pompeii on p. 34 of the students' textbook provides an initial view of the physical features and pattern of the town. Use the pictures in this Stage and on pp. 43, 65, 109, 127, and 148 to take the students on a visual "walking tour" of Pompeii, emphasizing the role of the public buildings in community life. If you have access to them, the images on the website and the Course video documentaries will also be useful here. You should show not only major public buildings but also street scenes with public fountains and stepping-stones, the numerous bars for warm drinks and snacks (**thermopōlia**), and the bakeries (**pistrīna**). If appropriate, encourage students to imagine Caecilius or Grumio showing a friend around the town. Students may need help in appreciating the size of the town: 163 acres means that the town was about half a mile square. It is worth comparing this measurement with a local park, the school grounds, or some other familiar space. Students may be puzzled by the white plaques visible in illustrations of the town. These were set up by archaeologists to provide a reference system for their grids and maps.

Discussion points might include:
1 Comparison with a modern town, highlighting similarities (large sports buildings, prevalence of graffiti) and differences (volume of traffic, absence of street names).
2 Amenities including entertainments, open spaces, transport, home lighting, water supply, transmission of news, cooking facilities, keeping warm or cool as needed.

Further information. The nationalities of Syphax and Pantagathus illustrate how cosmopolitan Pompeii was because of its mercantile contacts with east and west, and because its development included occupation by Etruscans, Greeks, and Samnites before the Romans. If you want to outline the history of the growth and development of Pompeii, this information is available from many sources.

Civic pride was strong and was expressed in public buildings, statues, inscriptions, and the civic deity, Venus Pompeiana. Many public buildings were erected by individuals at their own expense. The people of Pompeii thrived on trade and industry and enjoyed a comfortable, even luxurious, lifestyle.

Most buildings had been badly damaged by the earthquake in AD 62 or 63. Some, including the temples of Venus and Jupiter, were still in ruinous condition; others, including the amphitheater, had been restored; private houses were repaired to an unprecedented standard of luxury and a new and very large bath complex, the Central Baths, had been started.

Illustrations

p. 33   A status symbol for the Romans was a seaside villa on the Bay of Naples. This small landscape suggests how tightly packed villas could be. It is a wall painting from the lavishly decorated tablinum of Marcus Lucretius Fronto in Pompeii.

p. 34   The photograph shows a Pompeian street with stepping-stones worn with use, ruts from wheeled vehicles, and the height of the sidewalk on the far side.

p. 35　● Fountain in the Street of Shops (Via dell' Abbondanza). Notice also the house preserved up to the second floor. Unexcavated volcanic debris and soil lie behind the facades of many of these houses and stores.

● Bakery in Pompeii showing two biconical grain mills. Only the conical bottom stone remains from the front mill. The one behind is almost complete. The grain was fed into an opening in the top of a moveable stone which was shaped to rest over the bottom stone and was turned by a slave or animal by means of a handle fitted into the socket on the side. The flour ran out between the two stones and collected on the circular platform beneath. In the background is the semicircular opening of the oven in which charred round loaves of bread were discovered. This particular bakery is the bakery of Modestus.

p. 36　Stabiae Street looking south with well-preserved stepping-stones. The Stabiae Gate is visible at the end of the street. There is a water tower at front left.

pp. 36–37 *Streets of Pompeii.* Clockwise starting from mid-left:

● She-goat shop sign of a dairy near the forum.

● Cast of shop shutters, formed by pouring concrete into the space left by the rotted wood.

● Street corner in older part of town where the streets are not arranged on a regular grid pattern. The restored central building shows how extra space could be obtained in the upstairs rooms. This house was a brothel. The street signs are modern.

● Electoral slogans professionally painted. Exterior plaster walls were commonly painted red at the bottom and white at the top.

● A bar (**thermopōlium**) in Via dell' Abbondanza, with amphorae stacked in the corner. Sunk into the counter are three pottery containers for the food and beverages. In one of these pots the excavators found 603 sesterces, a fair sum, probably the last day's take. Painted on the wall behind is a lararium with Mercury, the god associated with profit (and thieves), at the far left, holding a purse.

● Wall painting from a small bar near the forum on the north side, not far from Caecilius' house.

● Holes in sidewalks are commonly found near doorways to houses and were probably used for tethering animals.

p. 38　Mercury, distinguished by his winged hat and characteristic herald's staff. One of five gods painted above a shop doorway in Via dell' Abbondanza.

Suggestions for further activities

1　On an outline plan of the town, fill in the key features: forum, theaters, amphitheater, palaestra, house of Caecilius, Stabian Baths, Forum Baths, main shopping area, sea gate, other gates. (This could be an individual project or you could use the board for a joint exercise with the whole class.)

2　Write or record a visitor's guide to Pompeii or design a travel poster or website, researching to amplify the material in the Stage.

3　Research the techniques of fresco painting. Produce a mural of either a scene from any book on Pompeii or a mythological scene, such as Hercules and the lion.

STAGE 4: in forō

Cultural context
The forum at Pompeii: finance and the law courts.

Story line
Caecilius lends money to a Greek merchant, Hermogenes, who does not repay the debt and is taken to court by Caecilius.

Main language features
● 1st and 2nd person singular present, including **sum, es**
e.g. *quid tū pingis? ego leōnem pingō.*

Sentence patterns
interrogative word (**quis, quid, cūr, ubi**) + NOM + V
e.g. *quid tū habēs?*
interrogative word + V + NOM
e.g. *quis es tū?*

Focus of exercises
1 Selection of suitable verb to match the subject in 1st or 2nd person singular.
2 **Story for translation.

Opening page (p. 39)

Illustration. View of the forum seen through the arch on the eastern side of the temple of Jupiter (opposite the view on p. 28). Part of the temple can be seen on the right. The brick buildings at the far end are the municipal offices. In the foreground, two stone blocks prevent wheeled traffic from entering the forum. The arch which frames the picture is made of brick-faced concrete but was originally faced with marble.

Model sentences (pp. 40–42)

New language feature. The 1st and 2nd person singular of the present tense. Familiar characters state in the first person who they are and what they are doing. They then answer questions posed to them in the 2nd person.

New vocabulary. ego, sum, vēndō, quid, tū, quis, es.

First reading. This presents little difficulty because the pictures give strong clues and there is little new vocabulary. Suggested procedure:
1 Teacher reads Grumio's statement (1) in Latin.
2 Teacher: Grumio is speaking. What does he say? (If necessary, act out the statement, emphasizing **ego**.)
3 Encourage use of the present progressive, e.g. *What are you selling?* (10) rather than *What do you sell?*
4 After the meaning has been elicited, give parts to individuals or groups. Ask them to read each pair of sentences aloud in Latin and then translate.

Note. ego and **tū** have been inserted in these sentences to aid students' recognition. They are gradually phased out in the Stages which follow.

Consolidation. A mime game is useful here. Students take turns in miming actions, and the class has to guess who they are or what they are doing (e.g. **tū es poēta** or **tū versum recitās**). If the class cannot guess, the student concerned has to tell them (e.g. **ego sum poēta** or **ego versum recitō**).

Hermogenēs (p. 43)

Story. Caecilius lends money to Hermogenes, a Greek merchant. He requires the transaction to be recorded on a wax tablet with the imprint of the merchant's seal. Hermogenes does not repay the loan.

First reading. Read the story at one sitting, leaving the students eager to find out what happens next.

The 1st and 2nd person singular crop up naturally in the dialogue, but any further comment should be postponed until study of About the language (p. 45). If **ego pecūniam quaerō** (line 5) causes difficulty, remind students that when Caecilius went to the harbor to see Syphax (p. 31), we were told **Caecilius servum quaerit**. A reminder of the context of a word's previous occurrence is far more effective than looking up the word in the Vocabulary.

At the end of the story invite speculation about what will happen in court. In order to respond, and to understand the implications of what Caecilius says in line 10 (**ego cēram habeō. tū ānulum habēs?**), students will need to know about the Roman practice of recording business transactions on wax tablets. See Further information below.

Consolidation. Follow up with a dramatic reading, or recapitulate when introducing the next story, or postpone consolidation until **in basilicā** has been read and the incident can be dramatized in its entirety.

Further information. Seals were commonly carried as rings, as illustrated on p. 44. Wax tablets recording business transactions (illustrated on pp. 9 and 47) were usually bound together in a set of three (i.e. six sides) as follows:

Front cover. Plain wood with title inscribed in ink.

Sides 2 and 3. Agreement or receipt in full, engraved in wax.

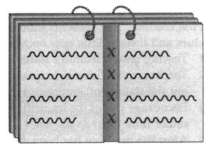

Side 4. Special leaf for signatures, with a fairly wide groove down the center. The two tablets were tied together down the middle with string and fastened along the groove with wax. The participants and witnesses would each press their seal into the wax down the center and sign their name across the leaf using both sides of the groove. In the illustration on the right, **X** represents the seal.

Side 5. Summary, giving brief details and names from the main text, possibly for reference, to enable the main text to remain sealed, or in case of loss.

Back cover. Usually plain wood.

The complete triptych was then bound around the outside.

Caecilius' surviving business records are of this type and are the main source for our knowledge about him. Encourage students to suggest modern analogies, like the rubber-stamped seals used by registered public accountants to certify the transactions they witness.

Illustration. Looking toward the arch from where the photograph on p. 39 was taken. In front of the row of shops stood a colonnade, which was roofed to give protection from the heat and glare of the sun. The row of pedestals inside the colonnade would have supported statues of prominent citizens. The columns have been partly reconstructed in brickwork in modern times.

in basilicā (p. 44)

Play. Caecilius takes Hermogenes to court and wins his case on the evidence of the wax tablet and the signet ring.

First reading. Set the scene and establish the court procedures by asking comprehension questions on lines 2–11. Then tell students to explore the meaning in groups of five, in preparation for assuming the characters of narrator, judge, Caecilius, Hermogenes, and his friend.

Check the students' understanding of the meaning and help them to envisage the scene and to reflect on the characters by asking, e.g.:

What do you think Caecilius does at line 26?

Why does Hermogenes say **ēheu!** in line 27? How loudly do you think he says it?

What is Hermogenes doing in line 29 when Caecilius says **ecce!**? Why?

What does the judge do in line 30 before saying **ānulus rem probat**?

Consolidation. Once students have an understanding of the story, draw attention to the illustrations of the basilica (p. 46), and the trial and writing tablet (p. 47).

Students can then be divided into groups and perform the play, either in English or in Latin. Students might be encouraged to record their performances. After all the productions are completed, the recordings can be played to the whole class and students vote for the best performers and the best play.

Illustrations. Clockwise from left:
- Enlarged image of peridot (semiprecious stone) seal engraved with horse (*Cambridge, Fitzwilliam Museum*).
- Seal ring made in gold without jewels (*London, Victoria and Albert Museum*).
- An amethyst with Medusa's head (*London, British Museum*).
- A carnelian showing Hygeia, goddess of health (*British Museum*).
- An onyx showing a warship (*British Museum*).

About the language (p. 45)

New language feature. 1st and 2nd person singular of the present tense.

Discussion. Ask students what they have noticed in the model sentences. Most will mention **ego** and **tū**; some will have spotted the new verb endings. See what progress they make with the formulation of rules; then proceed with the language note.

Consolidation. Follow the initial reading with oral practice of other familiar verbs. Retain **ego** and **tū**, or use a noun as subject for the time being. When students appear confident, follow up with further oral practice in the 1st and 2nd person with the subject omitted.

Practicing the language (pp. 46–47)

Exercise 1. Selection of suitable verb to match the subject in 1st or 2nd person.

**Exercise 2.* Story. Grumio comes home drunk and is frightened by the mural of a lion in the dining room.

Exercise 1 provides practice on the new language feature, while exercise 2 provides an example of the type of story creative teachers can compose for review and/or testing. When composing your own stories, be sure to use only sentence patterns the students are familiar with and to set the story in the appropriate cultural context. Students should expect to learn about Roman culture through their reading in Latin.

Illustrations

p. 46   As can be seen from the aerial photograph on p. 51, the basilica was vast. Its roof timbers were supported on twenty-eight brick pillars lining the central space. Students may recognize the central nave and side aisles as the architectural feature of a Christian basilica. Like the walls, the pillars were covered in stucco and painted to look like marble. The rectangular object is the base of an equestrian statue.

p. 47   • Detail of a painting from Pompeii which shows the judgment of Solomon or a parallel story. Two soldiers watch as a woman kneels before a judge on the tribunal. On either side of him is an advisor (*Naples, Archaeological Museum*).

      • Wax tablet as described on p. 42 of this manual (*Naples, Archaeological Museum*).

Cultural context material (pp. 48–51)

Content. The physical appearance of the forum and the range and importance of the activities which occurred there.

Suggestions for discussion. A single location for state ceremonial, law, religion, administration, business, and daily shopping will be a strange concept for many students. Discussion of the question, "Is there a modern equivalent?" will enable them to draw on their own experience of village green, town market square, or urban shopping center, and examine the significance of the Pompeian evidence more closely for similarities.

Illustrations

p. 48   • Part of a colonnade on west side of forum. The lower story is Doric, the upper Ionic, which, following Greek tradition, is more slender.

      • Line drawing based on a frieze (from the atrium of the House of Julia Felix) showing scenes in the forum. Photographs of other scenes from the same frieze are on pp. 49 and 144 (*Naples, Archaeological Museum*).

      • Marble statue of Eumachia, with traces of paint visible on the hair. It was found in the building she financed.

p. 49   • Photograph of the same frieze as that on p. 48 (see above).

      • Equestrian statue (restored). This comes from Herculaneum. No statues were found in the forum at Pompeii, either because they had been removed for restoration after the earthquake which occurred in AD 62 or 63, or because they were recovered by survivors after the eruption (*Naples, Archaeological Museum*).

p. 50   Scroll of plant forms inhabited by birds. Fine decoration carved in marble on the doorway of Eumachia's building.

p. 51   The aerial photograph of the forum is surrounded by details of some of the principal buildings. The notes below are numbered to match the photograph. Those that refer also to the surrounding illustrations have headings printed in **boldface**.

  1   **Temple of Jupiter**, flanked by two triumphal arches.

2 **The market hall (macellum)** had little shops along its walls inside and out, with the fish market at the back. In the middle of the central courtyard was a water tank. The **forum olitōrium** (vegetable market) was located across the forum behind the colonnade. As well as in such specialized market buildings, vendors would set up small stalls in the open space of the forum and in the porticoes.

3 Temple of the Lares of Pompeii, possibly built in expiation after the earthquake of AD 62 or 63.

4 **Temple of the Emperors**, dedicated to the cult of the most recent emperor. At the time of the eruption in AD 79 this was Vespasian, who had died two months earlier.

5 Eumachia's building was donated by the wealthy priestess and patroness of the clothworkers, Eumachia (p. 48) and may have been a market, perhaps of the clothworkers. This association may have been the largest business group in the town and played an influential part in local politics. No fewer than twenty-four electoral notices for AD 79 mention a fuller.

6 Polling station, situated at the end of the Via dell' Abbondanza. Voting in the municipal elections took place here annually.

7 **The municipal offices**, occupied by the duoviri, the aediles, and the decurions, or council, with their staff of clerks and officials. In front of the offices was a colonnade, shown in the picture. (Local government is discussed in Stage 11.)

8 The basilica was not only the courthouse but also the financial center, rather like a modern Stock Exchange.

9 **Temple of Apollo**, where Apollo and Diana were worshipped. The **cella** was raised on a high podium in the central courtyard, with an altar at the foot of the steps and a sundial on a tall pedestal at one side. The statues of Apollo and Diana (which are copies) face each other across the courtyard.

10 **The weights and measures table (mēnsa ponderāria)** in a recess on the forum side of the courtyard of the temple of Apollo. Cut into the stone slab was a series of cavities of different sizes in which purchasers could measure the grain or foodstuffs they had bought to ensure that they had been sold the correct quantity. The cavities had plugs and holes in the bottom to allow foodstuffs to be collected easily.

p. 52 Detail of carving on **larārium** from Caecilius' house showing a scene during the earthquake of AD 62 or 63. The temple of Jupiter has an altar in front of it and equestrian statues on either side. The artist has shown only four of the six columns which formed the colonnade at the front of the temple. The scene may commemorate the survival of the family in the earthquake (cf. pp. 166–167).

Suggestions for further activities

1 Construct a frieze of the forum as a pedestrian precinct surrounded by colonnades and buildings. Different groups could be allocated different areas and could use information from later Stages and further research to complete the task over a period of time.

2 Create exercises in historical empathy (e.g. written account, audio or video recording, dramatic presentation) to develop the characters, e.g. Clemens bargaining for food in the forum, or Caecilius negotiating a business deal in Eumachia's building.

3   Supply a ground plan of the forum and ask students to number the buildings on the plan:

        1   Temple of Jupiter
        2   Market
        3   Temple of the Lares of Pompeii
        4   Temple of the Emperors
        5   Eumachia's building
        6   Polling station
        7   Municipal offices
        8   Basilica
        9   Temple of Apollo
       10   Table of weights and measures

4   If appropriate, compare Pompeii and your town (colonnaded buildings, statues, churches, main square or city center, Latin inscriptions, graffiti, arches, etc.), perhaps building up a photo collage.

5   Make seal rings from plaster or fast-drying clay.

Vocabulary checklist (p. 52)

ānulus is the root for the English derivative "annular," which is spelled with two "n"s, e.g. an annular eclipse.

   coquit gives us the word "biscuit," literally meaning cooked/baked twice.

   habet means *have* (cf. **taberna**/*tavern*).

   quaerit gives us the English word "query." The Latin diphthong **ae** comes into English as "e." Knowing this may help students recognize the Latin roots of some English words.

   You should also pronounce carefully both "d"s of **reddit**, i.e. **red-dit** (from **reddere**), or students may fall into the bad habit of confusing it with **redit**, a different verb that means *returns* (from **redīre**).

STAGE 5: in theātrō

Cultural context
The theater: actors and performances;
pantomime, comedy.

Story line
Play attended by all Caecilius' household.
Poppaea, a slave girl, has trouble persuading
her master, Lucrio, to go to the theater so that
she can meet Grumio.

Main language features
- nominative plural
  e.g. *puellae sunt in viā.*

- 3rd person plural present
  e.g. *senēs ad theātrum ambulant.*

Sentence patterns
NOM et NOM + V
e.g. *fēminae et puellae sunt in turbā.*

Focus of exercises
1 Agreement of verb with nominative
   plural.
2 Agreement of verb with nominative
   singular and plural.
3 **Story for translation.

From this Stage onwards teachers should refer to the general notes on teaching method
in the Introduction if no specific guidance is given about the handling of the model
sentences or stories.

Opening page (p. 53)

Illustration. Detail of Pompeian wall painting showing tragic mask. The mask represents
Oceanus, hence the unusual color (*Naples, Archaeological Museum*). Vivid and dramatic
wall decoration was fashionable. Whole rooms were painted with brightly colored
spectacular scenes of theatrical fantasy (see also p. 15).

Model sentences (pp. 54–57)

New language feature. Plural of nouns and verbs. In this Stage only the nominative
plural of nouns is introduced, with the 3rd person plural of the present tense. (The
accusative plural is introduced in Stage 8.)

**New vocabulary. sunt, puella, puer, in theātrō, spectātor, āctor, in scaenā, fēmina,
iuvenis, plaudit.**

Illustrations. Street scenes depicting in simplified form the Via dell' Abbondanza east of
the intersection with the Via di Stabia. The theater is about 200 yards (180 meters) away.

The theater shown in the drawing at the top of p. 56 is the large open-air one with
5,000 seats shown in the photograph on p. 65. This theater has an elaborate permanent
stone set, with statues framed by two tiers of columns. Traces remain of a slot along
the front of the stage from which a stage curtain (**sīparium** or **aulaea**) could be raised.
The drawing depicts the canvas awning suspended from wooden poles set in sockets
around the top of the walls and stretched across the audience by ropes. The effect of the
light filtering through awnings into the auditorium is described by Lucretius (*De rerum
natura* IV.75–83):

> *When gold, red, or orange awnings flap and flutter, stretched over great theaters,
> hung from poles and beams, they have a way of broadcasting their own color. For*

they tinge the tiers of seats below, the whole stage, and the fashionable throng, and make them ripple with their own hue.

The other drawings depict an audience seated in the smaller roofed theater shown in the photograph on p. 64. The stage of this theater has a plain back wall and could have accommodated painted scenery.

āctōrēs (p. 58)

Story. The passage describes the effect of the arrival in Pompeii of two well-known actors, Actius and Sorex.

First reading. Guide the class through the story carefully, because there are many new words and phrases. Comparison with modern celebrities will help the class to capture the mood of the passage. A bronze bust of Sorex is shown on p. 64, and a graffito referring to Actius is quoted on p. 65.

Students enjoy speculating on the reason why Grumio stays behind in the house (lines 13–14) before they find out in the next story.

Consolidation. Rereading in different ways (see p. 13 of the Introduction) is important in helping students to absorb the plural forms and the vocabulary.

Illustrations

p. 58   Two actors representing a man (left) and woman from comedy. The statues were originally brightly colored and stood in the garden of a house near the two theaters at Pompeii (*Naples, Archaeological Museum*).

p. 60   The tragic actor, from a Pompeian wall painting, is reflecting on the character he will act (*Naples, Archaeological Museum*).

About the language 1 (pp. 59–60)

New language feature. Plurals. The change from singular to plural is presented in the context of the whole sentence.

Discussion. Elicit the following points:

1   Sentences referring to more than one person or thing are plural.
2   They use a different form of words.
3   Both noun and verb show the difference between singular and plural. Let the students see that the same thing occurs in English, e.g. get them to pluralize "The dog barks," and ask them how many words change.

For the moment concentrate on the verb endings in paragraph 3. Detailed consideration of noun endings is postponed until About the language 2 (p. 62). Do not at this stage introduce the additional complication of the variation between conjugations. This is explained in the Language information section of the textbook (pp. 184–185).

The irregularity of **esse** (p. 60, paragraph 4) may cause problems. Compare with English "am," "is," "are," and forms in Spanish, French, etc. Since students have already met all three singular forms of this verb, such comparisons should help demonstrate how regular its irregularities are.

Consolidation. Refer the class to **āctōrēs** (p. 58) and ask them to pick out singular and plural verb forms.

Poppaea (p. 61)

Play. A new character, Poppaea the slave girl, has difficulty persuading her aged master, Lucrio, to go to the theater so that she can receive a visit from her boyfriend, Grumio.

First reading. Prepare for a dramatized reading by questioning the students about the atmosphere in Pompeii and the attitudes of the characters. The appearance of Grumio makes a satisfying climax and provides the answer to students' speculations.

Consolidation. The dramatized reading requires four characters (narrator, Poppaea, Lucrio, **amīcus**/Grumio) and groups (or the whole class) for **agricolae** and **puerī**.

Discussion of the contextual information on "The comedies of Plautus" (pp. 66–67) may be useful in defining stock characters (old man, pretty slave girl, and wily slave) and the elements of intrigue and trickery. The play **Poppaea** can be seen as a simplified illustration of these features.

About the language 2 (p. 62)

New language feature. Nominative plural with 3rd person plural.

Discussion. The focus is mainly on nouns. As students gain confidence, some examples of other nouns from previous stories could be listed on the board, e.g. **agricolae**, **nautae**, **puerī**, **āctōrēs**, **iuvenēs**, as long as they are seen initially in the context of a complete sentence.

Then move on to paragraph 5 and revise the -**t** and -**nt** inflections of the verb. As with the nouns, further examples from the stories can be highlighted, e.g. **labōrant**, **intrant**, **currunt**, **ambulant**, **contendunt**.

Consolidation. Write on the board additional singular and plural sentences of the NOM + V pattern. Ask the students to translate these sentences and then to point out the nominative singulars and nominative plurals, using verb endings as clues or confirmations.

Practicing the language (p. 63)

Exercise 1. Agreement of verb with nominative plural.

Exercise 2. Agreement of verb with nominative singular and plural.

**Exercise 3.* Story. The Pompeians are in the theater watching a play, which they desert for a performance by a tightrope walker. The story is based on an incident described in Terence's *Hecyra* Prologue 4.

Cultural context material (pp. 64–67)

Content. The material explains the part played by the theater in Pompeian life and describes the theaters in Pompeii and the plays put on in them.

Suggestions for discussion. Both text and illustrations are best introduced at the point where they relate to the linguistic material, e.g. "The theater at Pompeii" with the model sentences on p. 56, and "The comedies of Plautus" with **Poppaea** on p. 61.

Further information. The theater was an established feature of life in the Roman republic, when the comedies of Plautus and Terence and some of the old Roman tragedies were regularly performed. Under the empire, most towns had a theater, where performances were most frequently pantomimes, vulgar farces, and one-act plays, with an occasional Plautine comedy. Although the crowds who came out in Pompeii to welcome actors like Actius and Sorex did not expect or desire entertainment of great dramatic quality, students should remember that, in Pompeii, the small covered theater, or **ōdēum**, was built during the Augustan period for more serious performances of music and poetic recitations. This theater would attract support from the more educated elements of Pompeian society.

The place in Pompeii's theater occupied by women is uncertain; we cannot be sure that segregation was observed in Pompeii as well as Rome.

Illustrations

p. 64
- Bronze head of Sorex found in temple of Isis in Pompeii (*Naples, Archaeological Museum*).
- The Odeon or small theater or roofed theater, Pompeii. This theater was meant for refined entertainment, such as musical performances, poetry recitals, and mime. The seating capacity is about 1,500 (cf. p. 56).

p. 65
- Large, open-air theater, Pompeii (cf. p. 56). A temporary stage and some wooden seats have been installed for modern performances.
- A masked musician dancing and playing a tambourine, from the villa of Cicero outside Pompeii. Other musicians play double pipes (shown in illustrations on pp. 67–68). This small mosaic has exceptionally fine tesserae and is signed by Dioscorides of Samos (*Naples, Archaeological Museum*).

p. 66 A popular type of terracotta mask, unlikely to have been worn in action, despite the holes for fastening, but used as an ornament (*Cologne, Römisch-Germanisches Museum*).

p. 67 The sequence of pictures represents a standardized comic plot.
- Marble relief of scene from comedy (*Naples, Archaeological Museum*).
- Detail of woman's mask from mosaic of theatrical masks from Hadrian's Villa. Masks overemphasized the features of the various characters to define their personalities. Note the double pipe behind the mask (*Rome, Capitoline Museums*).
- The slave has been attending his young master at a party as can be seen from the wreath he is wearing. Terracotta statuette (*London, British Museum*).
- Most comedies have a recognition scene to bring about their denouement. Fragment of mosaic (*Naples, Archaeological Museum*).

p. 68 Detail from Pompeian wall painting. Satyr dancing on a **thyrsus**, the wand carried by followers of Dionysus (*Naples, Archaeological Museum*).

Suggestions for further activities

1   Research, for written, oral, or video reports, the history of the Greek and Roman theater, both physical and literary.
2   Discuss a modern television program with some of the characteristics of Roman comedy and explain its popular appeal.
3   Give a dramatic reading or performance of a scene from a Roman comedy in translation.
4   Using heavy paper or even a plaster mold, draw and color a theatrical mask using the illustrations in the Stage.
5   Show a clip from *A Funny Thing Happened on the Way to the Forum*, a pastiche of plots from *Pseudolus*, *Casina*, *Miles Gloriosus*, and other plays by Plautus.

Vocabulary checklist (p. 68)

The imperative form of **adest** is found in the traditional Latin Christmas song "Adeste, Fideles!"

agricola comes from the Latin words **ager** meaning "field" and **colō** meaning "cultivate."

hodiē comes from the Latin words **hōc** and **diē** meaning "on this day," hence *today*.

"Rejuvenate" is a derivative of **iuvenis**. Note that the Latin **i** consonant comes into English as a **j**. The Latin **i** is usually a consonant when it is an initial letter followed by a vowel, or when it occurs between two vowels.

ubi gives us "ubiquitous" via the Latin word **ubīque** meaning "everywhere."

STAGE 6: Fēlīx

Opening page (p. 69)

Illustration. Relief showing manumission ceremony. The magistrate stands holding the
rod with which he has freed two former slaves. The conical felt cap (**pilleus**) which each
is wearing is a mark of his new status as a freedman. The standing freedman appears to
be shaking hands with his master whose figure has been lost from the right side of the
relief; the other one is kneeling to him in gratitude (*Morlanwelz, Belgium, Musée royal
de Mariemont*).

Model sentences (pp. 70–71)

New language feature. Introduction of two past tenses, perfect and imperfect, in the
3rd person. In this Stage, the perfect tense has only the form in **v**, e.g. **clāmāvit**. The
imperfects **erat** and **erant** are also introduced.

New vocabulary. timēbat, superāvit, pulsāvit (*punched*).

First reading. There is no signal in the text to indicate the change to past time. However,
if the teacher carefully uses comprehension questions set in the past, the students will
readily follow suit, e.g. *Sentence 1*: "What were the slaves doing?"

Experience indicates that students are likely (in fact, almost relieved) to translate
sentences about a past Pompeii in the past tense.

In English, as in Latin, it is characteristic for the imperfect to be used in describing a
situation, and the perfect to represent a momentary happening. The pairs of sentences
highlight the contrast between the situation and the action which interrupts it, e.g. "The
slaves *were walking* when the dog *barked*."

Initially, it is sufficient for the students to see the difference in terms of their English
translation. It is helpful to use consistently forms like "were walking" and "was annoying"
for the imperfect, wherever possible, moving gradually toward a more flexible approach

in later Stages, as students gain confidence in recognizing the forms. It may help to have some of the sentences and their translations on the board in two columns, one for each tense.

Consolidation. Encourage students to create some simple rules of their own for recognizing and translating the tenses. Students will be more likely to remember and use principles which they have worked out for themselves. They will probably work out that the endings -**bat** and -**bant** correspond to the English forms "was -ing" and "were -ing" and that **v** denotes the shorter form of the past tense, e.g. "walked," "shouted." To help students internalize the concept of imperfect and perfect, you might have volunteers act out **pulsābat/pulsāvit**, **lātrābat/lātrāvit**, etc.

pugna (p. 72)

Story. Clemens is strolling in the forum observing the activities around him when a fight breaks out between a farmer and a Greek merchant.

First reading. This passage contains descriptions of situations interrupted by momentary actions. You can reinforce the difference between the perfect and the imperfect by using such questions as:

> Where was Clemens walking?
> What was in the forum?
> Who were buying food?
> What did the farmer do to the Greek merchant?
> What were the Pompeians doing?
> Why did Clemens hurry when he heard the noise?
> Which Latin word tells you the fight went on for some time? (**tandem**)
> Why do you think the Pompeians supported the farmer?

quod and **postquam** occur here for the first time, and sentences become longer. It is helpful if students listen to and then repeat these sentences in Latin, stressing the pauses at the comma boundaries and getting the intonation right. It takes time for students to master **quod** and **postquam**.

Consolidation. When the students have understood the story, ask them to produce translations individually, or in pairs or groups, and then compare and discuss the variations. This process provides another opportunity to highlight the two tenses.

This story is perhaps the first to present an unpleasant aspect of life in Pompeii: racism or xenophobia. You may wish to play down this troublesome characteristic if it is a touchy subject in your school. Otherwise, you can use the story as a springboard for investigating the history of Pompeii and the natural resentment between the various peoples who, in turn, exercised control over the area, a resentment mirrored, alas, in many modern societies, including our own.

Fēlīx (p. 72)

Story. Clemens meets Felix in a bar and takes him home, where he is welcomed by Caecilius and Metella, and moved by seeing Quintus.

First reading. Use the question and answer technique. Possible questions are to be found on p. 13 of the Introduction.

An emotional moment occurs in lines 9–10 (**paene lacrimābat; sed rīdēbat.**). Encourage the class to recognize the feelings and speculate on the reasons for them. The explanation emerges in the next story. If students find **lacrimābat** difficult because the nominative is omitted, ask them what the meaning of **lībertus ... lacrimābat** would be and then the meaning without the noun.

Similarly, students might reflect on Grumio's happiness in line 13. Had Felix been a good friend of Grumio when he was a member of Caecilius' household?

Fēlīx et fūr (p. 73)

Play. Felix and Caecilius explain to Quintus how Felix earned his freedom.

First reading. At the end of the story, remind students of the emotion shown by Felix in lines 9–10 of the previous story, so that they can reflect on the relationships revealed by his feelings.

Consolidation. If this story is acted, the content of Caecilius' second speech can be mimed. You will need five actors: Caecilius, Quintus, Felix, the baby, and the thief. Discussion about character and situation provides the stimulus to study the information about slaves and freedmen (pp. 78–81). This is also a good story to represent as a cartoon, using sentences from the story as captions.

About the language (pp. 74–75)

New language features. Imperfect and perfect tenses (**v**-stems) in 3rd person singular and plural; **erat** and **erant**.

Discussion. Gather together the rules which students have evolved with you so far and introduce the language note as a development of their own ideas. Read paragraphs 1–4.

Consolidation. Reinforce immediately with oral translation of further examples on the board. Use only complete sentences and present one contrast at a time, e.g.:

1   **Caecilius in tablīnō labōrābat. servī in hortō labōrābant.**
    Caecilius in viā ambulābat. Caecilius et Quīntus in viā ambulābant.
    spectātōrēs erant in theātrō. āctor erat in scaenā.
    (*imperfect singular* with *imperfect plural*)
    Use the same verb in both halves of your first examples to keep distractions to a minimum (e.g. **labōrābat ... labōrābant; ambulābat ... ambulābant**). Later you can change the verb, keeping the contrast consistent, as in the following examples:

2   **īnfāns in cubiculō dormiēbat. fūr per iānuam intrāvit.**
    mercātor pecūniam nōn reddēbat. Caecilius mercātōrem ad basilicam vocāvit.
    (*imperfect singular* with *perfect singular*)

3   **cīvēs ad theātrum contendēbant. nūntiī fābulam nūntiāvērunt.**
    (*imperfect plural* with *perfect plural*)

Now read paragraphs 5 and 6, which introduce the ideas of continuous and momentary or completed action. Test the students' grasp of these distinctions by asking them about the contrasting verbs in the examples from **2** and **3** above.

Illustration. Bar at Herculaneum. The woodwork survives remarkably well. Visible are the railing of a mezzanine floor, a rack containing eight amphorae suspended from the wall, and large storage jar buried in the ground, left.

Practicing the language (pp. 76–77)

Exercise 1. Story with comprehension questions. Thieves intending to rob a miser of his money are thwarted by his faithful slave, a snake. The level of difficulty of the story is the same as in the main reading passages, and the new language features are included. You may need to help students with their first reading, and judge when they are ready to tackle comprehension questions.

Exercise 2. Agreement of nominative singular and plural with verb and additional practice in translating imperfect and perfect.

Illustration. Cobra, detail from Pompeian wall painting (*Naples, Archaeological Museum*).

Cultural context material (pp. 78–81)

Content. The institution of slavery; the work and treatment of slaves; **manūmissiō**; freedmen and freedwomen.

Suggestions for discussion. It is useful to introduce the material in the context of the stories, **Fēlīx** (p. 72) and **Fēlīx et fur** (p. 73), where it illuminates character and relationships. Discussion can start from the familiar situation, e.g.:

> What relationship does there seem to be between Caecilius and his slaves?
> What sort of jobs did the slaves in his household perform?
> What aspects of Grumio's life as a slave might he dislike?
> What compensations might he find in it?
> What might Felix say to Grumio about his life as a freedman?

It can then develop toward a wider view, and greater realism, e.g.:

> What other work was done by slaves in Pompeii?
> What difficulties would face a young person brought from a distant country into slavery in Roman society?

The topic will be further explored later in the Course.

Further information. Since there is no parallel in present-day western society, and slavery in other societies had a different rationale, slavery needs to be explained in terms of actual Roman practice. This is complex because the condition and role of Roman slaves varied at different times and places and with different masters, ranging from a relationship of respect and mutual confidence to resentment and extreme brutality. It is important to help the students distinguish between racism and slavery in your discussion. Color or ethnic origin did not signify slavery or inferiority. Not all blacks were slaves; many were free men who, with their families, had emigrated as mercenary soldiers. The majority of slaves came from wars in provinces other than in the African continent and would have been fair skinned. There was, in practice, very little difference between a slave and a poor free man. Snowden offers an excellent collection of illustrations of blacks from wall paintings, vases, etc. He argues that careful examination of such paintings and of original Latin texts points to a relatively favorable image of blacks and of a good black–white relationship in the ancient world. However, more recently Isaac has argued for proto-racist attitudes in the Roman world based on geographical and environmental factors, citing for instance comments by Livy and Cicero that the Syrians were born for slavery (Livy 35.98, 36.17; Cicero's *de provinciis consularibus* 5.10).

Students often ask about the cost of slaves. The normal range in the first century AD was approximately 800–8,000 sesterces, but especially attractive or gifted slaves would be priced higher. The highest recorded price was 700,000 sesterces paid for the grammarian, Lutatius Daphnis, who was then immediately freed. Compare this with other prices of the time, e.g.:

1,200 sesterces (300 denarii) – legionary's annual pay

10,000 sesterces – highest permitted fee for lawyer

1,000,000 sesterces – property qualification for senator.

Under Augustus, a law was passed restricting the number of slaves that could be freed in a will and establishing thirty as the minimum age for manumission. It has been suggested that Augustus passed this law because the Romans feared that the excessive number of freedmen was diluting the body of pure Roman citizens. The very existence of such a law testifies to a relatively liberal practice of freeing slaves.

Illustrations

p. 78   Detail from lid of sarcophagus of AD 160–170 representing battle between Romans and Gauls (*Rome, Capitoline Museums*).

p. 79   • Slave serving drinks, from carving on third-century tomb from Neumagen. He stands by a table on which are an amphora and a wine-strainer (*Trier, Rheinisches Landesmuseum*).

• Nurse with baby in cradle from third-century memorial (*Cologne, Römisch-Germanisches Museum*).

• Top surface of lamp showing eight men carrying barrel slung from two shoulder poles (*London, British Museum*).

• Mosaic head, perhaps of gladiator, from Baths of Caracalla (*Rome, Museo Nazionale Romano*).

p. 80   Overseer beating man with cane, from Mosaic of the Great Hunt, Piazza Armerina, Sicily.

p. 81   The replanted peristyle garden from the House of the Vettii, Pompeii reveals the wealth acquired by many freedmen. The identity of the ancient plants was deduced from the holes left by their roots. In the summer, underground **fistulae** (lead pipes) are turned on to carry water to fountains and bird baths.

p. 82   Cupids drawn by deer in chariot race, in the triclinium of the House of the Vettii, Pompeii. The lavish frescoes testify to the wealth acquired by many freedmen.

Suggestions for further activities

1   You are Syphax composing an advertisement for selling a slave. Give details of name, age, nationality, previous history, skills, and price.

2   Write two imaginary letters from Felix, after gaining your freedom, **a** to Caecilius, and **b** to a fellow freedman. Consider the different points of view which you might express in these two letters.

Vocabulary checklist (p. 82)

"Redeem" is an example of the kind of derivative students have difficulty connecting with its Latin root, since **emit** is "buried" behind a prefix.

per gives us many English words, such as "percolate," "perforate," "permeate," "perspective."

rēs gives us "republic" from **rēs pūblica**, *the public thing*. **rēs** also gives us "real" and "reified." **rēs** is here translated as *thing* for the sake of simplicity, but discuss with students the range of meanings the word acquires in different contexts. So far students have met:

rem probat   *he proves the case* (p. 44, lines 24–25, 30).
rem nārrat   *he tells the story* (p. 73, line 3).
rem audit   *he hears the story* (p. 73, line 20).

To reinforce the point that words may have more than one possible translation, refer students to p. 192, paragraph 9.

The definition of "prescription," from **scrībit**, is a reminder that the "Rx" symbol associated with pharmacies was connected with the Latin word **recipit** from which our words "recipe" and "receipt" are derived.

STAGE 7: cēna

Cultural context
Roman burial customs; beliefs about life after death.

Story line
Caecilius and Metella's guests, already frightened by a werewolf story told after dinner and news of a missing guest's death, are terrified on their homeward journeys by the cry of a cat. Metella comforts Melissa who is upset by criticism from Grumio and Clemens.

Main language features
perfect tense (other than **v**-stems)
e.g. *amīcī optimum vīnum bibērunt. tandem surrēxērunt.*

Sentence patterns
ACC + v (i.e. nominative omitted/suppression of the subject)
e.g. *vīllam intrāvit.*

Focus of exercises
1 **Story with comprehension questions.
2 Selection of verbal phrase to match nominative.
3 Selection of nominative or accusative singular; nominative singular or plural.

Opening page (p. 83)

Illustration. Mosaic of a skeleton butler, holding a wine jug in each hand, found in a triclinium in Pompeii (*Naples, Archaeological Museum*). Romans often introduced images of death to their dining rooms as a reminder of the transience of life and the need to enjoy its pleasures while they could.

Model sentences (pp. 84–85)

New language features. Sentence pattern ACC + v (i.e. nominative omitted). Perfect tenses, with forms in **s**, **ss**, **x**, and **u**.

New vocabulary. pōculum, īnspexit, longam, hausit, valē. Also students may not connect the form **surrēxērunt** with **surgit**.

First reading. Establish the meaning with sequential comprehension questions, e.g.: *Sentence 2:* "What was Caecilius doing? What did *he* do next?" Then ask for the pair of sentences to be translated together.

fābula mīrābilis (p. 86)

Story. Felix entertains Caecilius and Metella's dinner guests with a story about a centurion who turns out to be a werewolf.

First reading. This is the first of three stories touching on the supernatural. Heighten the atmosphere by making the reading in Latin as dramatic as possible, and by choosing tantalizing points to break off and explore the meaning, e.g.:

> **Decēns nōn adest** (line 4)
> **... subitō centuriōnem cōnspexit** (line 10)
> **ingēns lupus subitō appāruit** (line 12).

We observed a class whose teacher turned out the lights and read the Latin by flashlight, rendering even more effective the wailing pronunciation of **ululāvit** (line 13).

Further information. The Romans were partial to stories of this kind and liked to tell them after dinner—the ancient equivalents of modern television fantasies about the supernatural. Belief in ghosts, however, as spirits of dead persons, was probably more widespread then than now. The original of **fābula mīrābilis** is found in Petronius, *Satyrica* 62. It illustrates the popular belief that a werewolf, if wounded, retains the wound even after he reassumes his human form.

Illustration. The atmospheric background for the werewolf is derived from a wall painting found in the temple of Isis (cf. p. 169), Pompeii (*Naples, Archaeological Museum*).

Note. There are minor differences between this story and the video dramatization.

About the language 1 (p. 87)

New language feature. Sentence pattern: ACC + V (i.e. nominative omitted).

Discussion. When students translate the examples in paragraph 4, they may need help with sentence **d**. If they translate **Grumiōnem salūtāvērunt** as *Grumio greeted them*, compare the sentence with **lībertī Grumiōnem salūtāvērunt**. If necessary, refer them to the sentences in paragraph 2. When students produce the correct translation, respond, "Yes, they greeted Grumio, but is there a word for 'they'? How can you tell that the sentence means, '*They* greeted Grumio'?" Analysis in terms of unexpressed nominative will not help most students, but many should now recognize that the **-em** termination of **Grumiōnem** indicates he could not have done anything, and that the **-nt** ending of **salūtāvērunt** is plural.

Consolidation. In designing further examples, use the device of paired sentences with the subject made explicit in the first sentence.

Illustration. Detail from a mosaic representing the unswept floor of a dining room (*Rome, Vatican Museums*). This design, based on a Hellenistic original, was popular in the ancient world.

Decēns (p. 88)

Play. Decens has failed to arrive for the dinner party. His slaves report his encounter with a ghostly gladiator, and Clemens' discovery of his body in the arena.

First reading. Some students find the story of the gladiator confusing, so make sure that they are clear about the events reported by the slaves.

Be prepared for heated discussion about the supernatural. Skeptics could be invited to find a rational reason for Decens' death.

Consolidation. Students, after their first reading of the story, can easily dramatize it. A narrator and five actors are needed; the entire class may add the **ēheu** at the news of Decens' death.

Exercises could be developed on several of the language features occurring in this story, e.g. the personal endings of the present tense and easily forgotten or confused words (**cōnspexit, valdē, tamen, petīvit, rem intellegō, ōlim**).

post cēnam (p. 89)

Story. The guests depart nervously, scattering noisily when alarmed by a cat. Caecilius and Metella sleep unperturbed.

First reading. While maintaining a mood of mystery, you should redouble in students their expectation of the unexpected, thus setting them up for the deliberate comedown of the howling cat. Most students will comprehend this short story without translating it, particularly if you ask effective comprehension questions, e.g. "Why were the friends advancing quietly through the town?" "What suddenly happened?" "How did this affect the friends?" etc.

After you have established the surface meaning, you might ask interpretive questions such as "Why did the caterwauling frighten Caecilius and Metella's friends so thoroughly?" "Why were Caecilius and Metella able to sleep so soundly?"

The content of this story does not bear repetition. It is appropriate sometimes to let one reading suffice, in order to demonstrate to students their growing competence and your confidence in them.

Illustrations

- Detail of stone mask decorating the courtyard of House of Neptune and Amphitrite in Herculaneum, photographed in a thunderstorm.
- Mosaic of cat with small bird. This was another popular theme in still-life paintings. This picture is made up of several thousand tiny pieces of colored stone each about .2 inches (5 mm) square. This version, similar to one found in the House of the Faun, Pompeii, is from a villa near Rome (*Rome, Museo Nazionale Romano*).

About the language 2 (p. 90)

New language feature. Further forms of the perfect.

Discussion

Paragraph 1. Students should recognize the perfect form in **v** which has already been explained in Stage 6. If necessary, list more examples from recent stories, reading the sentences aloud and writing up the verbs in the same format they are about to meet in paragraph 2, e.g.:

	PRESENT	PERFECT	
		singular	*plural*
omnēs ad ātrium festīnāvērunt.	festīnat	festīnāvit	festīnāvērunt
gladiātor clāmāvit.	clāmat	clāmāvit	clāmāvērunt

Paragraph 2. After discussing the new forms, guide students to supply further examples from the model sentences or the stories they have read, and add them to the list, e.g.:

omnēs plausērunt.	plaudit	plausit	plausērunt
dominus gladiātōrem cōnspexit.	cōnspicit	cōnspexit	cōnspexērunt

Note. Students may not have met or remembered the present tense of some of the new perfect forms.

Students are often adept at composing mnemonics. Ask them to invent mnemonics for the "key" letters of the perfect, i.e. **v, x, u, s**, and then vote for the best one.

Paragraph 3. Read with students the explanation about the listing of verbs on p. 191, paragraphs 4, 5, and 6. Ask them to do the examples in paragraph 7 (p. 192). Then explore with the students the new setup for verbs on the Vocabulary checklist (p. 98).

Illustration. Table-top mosaic of Death from a summer triclinium, Pompeii. Beneath the skull, a butterfly is a reminder that time flies. The wheel signifies the turning of time and fortune. Above the skull is a carpenter's level and plumb line. At the right is a poor wanderer's clothing, at the left an emperor's purple cloak. All are made level by death (*Naples, Archaeological Museum*).

Metella et Melissa (p. 91)

Story. Metella finds Melissa in tears because Grumio and Clemens have been angry with her. She comforts the slave girl by praising her work.

First reading. Contrast Metella's sympathetic treatment of Melissa with her earlier attitude (p. 31) and discuss the reasons for this change. How does Metella's behavior inform our impression of her?

The use of **heri** and **hodiē** will help students with the frequent changes of time. Where these indicators are lacking, you may need to use leading comprehension questions, e.g.: "What was Metella doing?" "What is the question she asks Grumio?"

Consolidation. Written translation of part of this story is a useful way of checking that students have learned to recognize the different tenses and personal endings. The story is also suitable for acting.

Practicing the language (pp. 92–94)

Exercise 1. Story with comprehension questions. Felix, Caecilius, and Quintus hunt a wild boar. When Felix' life is in danger, Quintus kills the boar and repays Felix for saving his life as a baby.

The predominance of new grammar features such as suppressed subject, adverbial clauses, and additional ways of forming the perfect tense will serve to test the students' understanding of these concepts. Monitor their progress and be prepared to assist those who are having difficulty. Discuss the story's happy ending: Quintus has a chance to repay Felix for saving his life and to display the spear-throwing agility that will serve him well when he saves King Cogidubnus in Stage 16. Also, since this is the only story illustrating the hunt as a leisure-time activity, you could discuss the details represented in the narrative.

Further information. Because hunting was one of the regular sports of nobles and other wealthy people, their sons would have been trained to ride horses and handle hunting weapons as soon as they were old enough. Remind students also that, before the eruption of AD 79, Vesuvius was heavily forested (illustration p. 173), an ideal setting for this story.

Illustration. Marble statue from the garden of the House of the Stags in Herculaneum.

Exercise 2. Selection of a phrase containing a verb in the perfect tense, to match a singular or plural nominative. Remind students of the endings -**t** and -**nt**. The last three examples are more difficult.

Exercise 3. Selection of nouns in the nominative or accusative singular and the nominative singular or plural. Explain to students that there are two points being practiced here and help them with a couple of examples, if necessary.

Cultural context material (pp. 95–97)

Content. Following the stories about the supernatural, this section gives a general picture of Roman beliefs about life after death and funerary practices.

Suggestions for discussion. Take care to discover beforehand if any student may, because of personal circumstances, find death a painful topic. If handled sensitively, discussion can be helpful on a number of levels. Questions for discussion and study include:

1   Why did most people in the ancient world die at a comparatively young age by modern western standards?
2   What memorials and customs kept the memory of the dead alive in Roman times? How different are these today?
3   Why may the excavation of tombs be helpful to archaeologists seeking to reconstruct the daily life of the time?
4   What modern beliefs are there about life after death?

Further information. Dupont calculates that 30 percent of Roman men and women reached the age of forty and 13 percent reached sixty, although census records list many cases of centenarians. Remember that only about 50 percent of children reached adulthood. The Romans were regularly reminded of the brevity of life and therefore gave considerable attention to the customs, memorials, and monuments by which they hoped posterity would remember them.

The exact funeral and burial rites varied according to historical period, social class, and local customs. Many people belonged to funeral clubs (**collēgia fūnerāticia**) which would pay the funeral expenses. The deceased from an upper-class family would first lie in state in the atrium. Then the deceased was carried on a bier through the streets in a funeral procession, organized by professional undertakers who provided mourning women and musicians. The procession might stop in the forum for a funeral oration (**laudātiō fūnebris**). If the family had held high political office (curule magistracies), members of the family, dressed as their ancestors and wearing the masks of the ancestors (**imāginēs**), were a prominent feature of the procession.

From the forum the procession moved outside the city to the grave or cremation site. In cremations, the Romans burned the dead on pyres. Gifts and personal possessions were sometimes burned as well. The ashes and bones were buried in a container of glass, metal, pottery, gold, or marble. At all times cremation and inhumation were practiced. After the mid-third century AD, inhumation became most common.

Students may be interested to know that many of the Roman customs are still traditional practices in Central and South America. In Aruba the crypts are built in the likeness and color of the houses of the deceased. In Mexico, from October 31st to November 2nd, the celebration of *Dia de los Muertos*, the Day of the Dead, includes family reunions with the dead. The relatives sweep and clean the graves, then have processions through the city to the graveyards, bringing flowers, candles, loaves of bread, and tequila for the souls of the departed.

Illustrations

p. 95 • Street of Tombs looking toward Herculaneum Gate, Pompeii. Note the variety of tomb designs. Tombs were usually situated by the side of important roads leading out of the town but were sometimes placed on rural estates.

   • Interior of a tomb in the Street of Tombs, with recesses for ashes. It probably belonged to Aulus Umbricius Scaurus, one of the most successful Pompeian manufacturers of **garum** (fish sauce), for which Pompeii was famous.

p.96 • Cylindrical lead canister buried in stone-lined pit. The stone is pierced by a feeding pipe (originally considerably longer) through which wine, milk, or honey could be poured (*Caerleon, Roman Legionary Museum*).

   • Amphorae from the cemetery at Isola Sacra, Ostia.

   • The Blue Vase. Like the Portland Vase, this was made using the cameo technique. A layer of white glass was applied over blue glass and then carved away to form the design of Cupids celebrating while harvesting grapes (*Naples, Archaeological Museum*).

p. 97 • A dining room, now poorly preserved, is shown in a nineteenth-century wood engraving. It has three masonry couches grouped around a circular table.

   • Head of Epicurus from Villa of the Papyri, Herculaneum (*Naples, Archaeological Museum*). This villa belonged to a wealthy Roman with a large library of Epicurean philosophical works, mostly in Greek. The Getty Villa in Malibu, California, is a reconstruction of this villa.

p. 98 Relief of wrongdoers punished in the underworld, from a sarcophagus (*Rome, Vatican Museums*).

Suggestions for further activities

1   Research and report on different philosophies current in Roman times. You might also be interested in reading and summarizing for the class Virgil's description of the underworld (*Aeneid* VI).

2   Research Roman superstitions in general (Paoli is especially thorough on this topic).

3   The Case of the Missing Guest. As a Roman investigating the death of Decens, write a report on your findings.

Vocabulary checklist (p. 98)

You will note that, starting with this checklist, verbs are presented in both their present and their perfect tenses, 3rd person singular. The English meaning is still given in the present tense. This pattern will continue for the rest of Unit 1.

   cum assimilates (**col-/com-/con-/cor-**) when joined as a prefix, e.g. "collaborate," "convention," "correspond."

   nihil comes from **nē**, meaning "not," and **hīlum**, "a trifle." If something is not even a trifle, then it is nothing.

   A "parasol" from **parō** is preparation for the sun.

STAGE 8: gladiātōrēs

Cultural context
The amphitheater and gladiatorial shows.

Story line
A senator called Regulus gives a gladiatorial show at Pompeii which ends in a riot. The story of Androcles and the lion.

Main language features
- accusative plural
  e.g. *puellae iuvenēs salūtāvērunt.*

- superlative adjectives
  e.g. *Pompēiānī erant īrātissimī, quod Rēgulus spectāculum rīdiculum ēdēbat.*

Focus of exercises
1 1st and 2nd person singular of present; accusative plural.
2 1st, 2nd, and 3rd person singular of present.
3 **Story for translation.

Opening page (p. 99)

Illustration. Top surface of a Roman clay lamp. This shows two fighters, bare-chested, each armed with helmet, pair of greaves, protection on sword arm, straight sword, and oblong shield. One contestant has dropped his shield (*Trier, Rheinisches Landesmuseum*).

Gladiators were a popular theme on lamps. The names of about twenty types of gladiator are known but few can be identified from the evidence of representations like this.

Model sentences (pp. 100–101)

New language feature. The accusative plural is now introduced within the basic sentence.

New vocabulary. spectāculum, nūntiābant, clausae, murmillōnēs, saepe, victōrēs.

First reading. Postpone comments on the formation of accusative plurals until students have read aloud and translated the sentences.

Consolidation. The illustrations can serve as an introduction to the cultural context topic of gladiators, if this has not already been done before reading the model sentences. The public announcements, the procession, the closed shops (a holiday), the physical setup of the amphitheater, the attendance of women, the salutation, and the different types of gladiator are all represented.

gladiātōrēs (p. 102)

Story. Regulus, a Roman senator who lives near Nuceria, puts on a gladiatorial show in the amphitheater at Pompeii since the Nucerians do not have an amphitheater of their own. The Pompeians are angered by the congestion caused by the influx of Nucerians, but initially calm prevails in the amphitheater.

First reading. This story needs careful planning because it presents a number of challenges. It contains little action but is important in setting the scene and creating the atmosphere for later stories in this Stage. There are some long sentences containing subordinate clauses introduced by **quod**, **postquam**, and **ubi**. Two contrasting strategies are:
1 To work on the material about gladiatorial shows (pp. 109–112) before reading this story, enabling the students to approach with more confidence the situations described in the Latin.

2 To give nothing away in advance but when reading the story heighten the students' awareness of impending trouble, e.g.:
- **erant inimīcī** (line 2)
- **saepe erant turbulentī** (line 4)
- **Nūcerīnī viās complēbant** (lines 7–8)
- **omnēs vehementer clāmābant** (line 15).

Longer Sentences. These usually follow an order which is familiar in English, but sometimes the subordinate clause is embedded in the main clause, e.g.:

Nūcerīnī, quod amphitheātrum non habēbant, saepe ad amphitheātrum Pompēiānum veniēbant (lines 3–4).

Pompēiānī, postquam nūntiōs audīvērunt, ad amphitheātrum quam celerrimē contendērunt (lines 13–14).

To give the students extra help here, you could:

1 Read the Latin sentences aloud with emphasis and appropriate pauses to demarcate the clauses.

2 After the first reading, break the complex sentence down into simple sentences for the students to translate, e.g.:

Nūcerīnī amphitheātrum nōn habēbant. Nūcerīnī saepe ad amphitheātrum Pompēiānum veniēbant.

and then knit it together again with the conjunction.

Illustration. Amphitheater at Pompeii, built in the first half of the first century BC, shown from the north. One of the external staircases gives access to seats at the top. The retaining wall encircles the embankment of earth which was created to support the seats by excavating the center of the arena. For illustration showing the interior, see p. 109.

in arēnā (p. 103)

Story. A contest between a pair of **rētiāriī**, supported by the Nucerians, and a pair of **murmillōnēs**, the Pompeians' favorites, is won by the retiarii. The retiarii exploit their superior mobility, the murmillones their superior equipment.

First reading. This can be a difficult story. Students often have a problem with the terms "retiarius" and "murmillo" and the whole story hinges on the difference between the two and their supporters. Notes, stick figures, and a diagram of the fight on the board can help here. Use comprehension questions to draw students' attention to the tactical elements, e.g.:

> Why did the retiarii at first avoid a fight?
> Were the Pompeians right to say that the retiarii were **ignāvī**?
> Why did the first murmillo attack the two retiarii on his own?
> Was this what the retiarii had been hoping for?

Consolidation. Change the focus of discussion to the reaction of the spectators, e.g.:

> Why did the Pompeians ask for mercy for the murmillones?
> What made the Nucerians demand their death?
> Why do you think Regulus sided with the Nucerians?

Illustration. A retiarius, armed with trident (in origin a fishing spear) and net, wearing a distinctive shoulder guard on his right shoulder. Relief from Chester (*Saffron Walden Museum*).

About the language 1 (p. 104)

New language feature. Accusative plural.

Discussion. You may wish to remind students of their first introduction to the accusative and the term "case" (p. 21), and the first chart of accusatives (p. 32).

After they have translated the examples in paragraph 4, ask them to indicate which word is in the accusative case and to give its number, e.g.:

> The slave girl praised the gladiator (**gladiātōrem** is *accusative singular*).
> The slave girl praised the gladiators (**gladiātōrēs** is *accusative plural*).

Consolidation. Students could:

1 Pick out examples of the accusative plural in stories they have already read.
2 Supply the Latin for words in English sentences by using the chart in the text, e.g.:
> Quintus greets *the girls*. Caecilius welcomes *the merchants*.

Extend this by mixing both singular and plural forms of the accusative.
3 Do further exercises on cases, being careful not to outpace the students' grasp of this new grammatical point. The stories and exercises to come will help consolidate their understanding.

vēnātiō (p. 105)

Story. The beast fight at Regulus' games. The uncharacteristic behavior of the lions on this occasion fuels the growing animosity between Pompeians and Nucerians, and a riot occurs.

First reading. Students should explore the complete story before attempting the comprehension questions. Give help, if necessary, with the complex sentences (see note on **gladiātōrēs** on p. 65 of the manual).

Consolidation. In further discussion of the story, the information about the riot (p. 113) will be useful. Students may wish to suggest various reasons why the lions fell asleep. (The Roman investigation did censure the Pompeians as well as Regulus.)

**pāstor et leō (p. 106)

Story. The story of the shepherd and the lion is based on Aulus Gellius' tale about Androcles and the lion (*Noctes Atticae* V.14.300).

First reading. This is a review passage containing examples of most of the noun and verb endings introduced so far, in particular the 1st and 2nd person of the present.

Consolidation. Students could draw a cartoon version of the story with suitable sentences selected as captions.

Illustration. Mosaic of seemingly unhappy lion (*Tunis, Bardo Museum*).

About the language 2 (p. 107)

New language feature. Superlative adjectives.

Discussion. Remind the students that this note sums up a linguistic feature which they first met in Stage 2 (at the end of the story **in triclīniō: Grumiō est laetissimus**) and which has occurred several times since.

Consolidation. Revisit in context regular superlatives which students have already met, e.g.:

> **Grumiō est laetissimus** (p. 20).
> **Pugnāx erat gladiātor nōtissimus** (p. 88).
> **canēs erant fortissimī, sed lupī facile canēs superāvērunt** (p. 105).
> **Nūcerīnī erant laetissimī** (p. 105).
> **tum Pompēiānī erant īrātissimī** (p. 105).

If students ask about **optimus**, which occurs very frequently, confirm that it is a superlative, but an irregular one. Compare English by asking the class if the superlative of "good" is "goodest." Postpone further discussion until Unit 2, where irregular comparatives and superlatives are presented.

Illustrations

- Wall painting from tomb of C. Vestorius Priscus who died aged twenty-two, three or four years before the destruction of the city. Note the hand raised in appeal for mercy (*Pompeii, in situ*).
- Two arena musicians playing curved horn and organ. The emotions of the spectators were heightened, as in a modern circus or sports competition, by musical accompaniment. Straight trumpets were also played (*Germany, third-century Roman villa at Nennig*).

Practicing the language (p. 108)

Exercise 1. Revision of 1st and 2nd person singular of present; further practice with accusative plural.

Exercise 2. Revision of the 1st, 2nd, and 3rd person singular or present (introduced in Stage 4).

***Exercise 3.* Story. Lucia and Melissa find a drunk freedman torturing a cat. When Lucia shouts at him to stop, the freedman threatens her, but she stands her ground and quickly thinks up a way to frighten the freedman off. This story helps to establish Lucia as courageous and quick-thinking.

Cultural context material (pp. 109–113)

Content. Description of the amphitheater and the kind of gladiatorial fights and beast hunts that took place in it; a translation of the account of the riot in the amphitheater at Pompeii (Tacitus, *Annals* XIV.17).

Suggestions for discussion. The amphitheater is an emotive subject. The reaction of students ranges from bloodthirsty pleasure to disgust and criticism. Although students should express what they feel, you should also make sure that they see the games in their historical context as a social institution, which—whatever we think about it—was an extremely popular leisure occupation. The following topics may help students to analyze the games further:

1   A comparison with modern forms of popular entertainment, including boxing, motor racing, bull fighting, and field sports (European soccer, North American football, or ice hockey). Similarities include the element of danger and violence. Differences include the fact that gladiators were normally aiming to kill each other and that they generally had no choice about participating.

2   The status of a gladiator compared with that of a racing driver or a matador. The love of danger and the adulation that inspire such dangerous sports might help explain why some gladiators, given their freedom, returned to the arena.

3   The reactions of the spectators, ranging from sadistic enjoyment to analytical appreciation of the performance of highly trained and skilled practitioners.

4   The fascination that violence has for people.

Further information. The amphitheater at Pompeii, built about 80 BC, is the earliest surviving amphitheater, predating the first permanent arena in Rome by fifty years. It was financed by the same **duovirī** who built the small theater. It seated about 20,000 spectators and measured 142 yards by 112 yards (130 x 102 meters). Inside there were three tiers of stone seats (**īma**, **media**, and **summa cavea**) and a barrier which separated the spectators from the arena. Outside there was an impressive series of blind arcades backed onto the containing wall and four staircases giving access to the **media cavea**.

It is uncertain whether the Augustan legislation requiring the segregation of men and women in the amphitheater applied or was policed outside Rome.

Roman gladiatorial shows usually took place in an amphitheater, occasionally in the forum, though there is no indication of this occurring in Pompeii.

There were four main types of contest in the arena: gladiators against gladiators, armed men against animals, animals against other animals, and unarmed men and women exposed to wild beasts.

Beast fights often provided a midday interlude at gladiatorial shows. Animals were matched against animals in a graded sequence, with progressively more powerful beasts released into the arena to fight and kill their predecessors. The same arrangement was sometimes employed with humans, each incoming gladiator being set against the winner of the previous fight.

The most recent scholarship on **pollicem vertit** confirms that raising the thumb up (toward the neck) was the signal for death while lowering the thumb down onto the closed fist was the gesture for mercy. See Corbeill.

Illustrations

p. 109 • Interior of amphitheater at Pompeii, viewed along long axis.
   • Detail from Pompeian wall painting showing the riot of AD 59. At the top is the awning (**vēlum** or **vēlārium**). People are fighting in the **arēna**, in the **cavea**, and outside (*Naples, Archaeological Museum*).

p. 110 Drawings based on stucco frieze in Pompeian tomb. Audience added by illustrator.

p. 111 • Pompeian statue of a Thracian gladiator, possibly used as a tavern sign, with a small statuette (to right) of the god Priapus. Thracians were armed with a small shield, either round (as here) or square, and a curved sword.
   • Examples of gladiator armor (*Naples, Archaeological Museum*).

p. 112 • Drawing based on same series of reliefs as drawings on p. 110.
   • Fragment of wall painting, similar to finds at Pompeii, from amphitheater at Merida, Spain, showing beast fighter with spear facing lioness (*Merida, National Museum of Roman Art*).

p. 113 • Drawing based on same wall painting as shown on p. 109.
   • Graffito showing victorious gladiator with palm, the symbol of victory; linked to the riot by writing below:

> CAMPANI VICTORIA VNA
>
> CVM NVCERINIS PERISTIS

Campanians, in your moment of victory you have perished along with the Nucerians. (Taking **ūnā** closely with **cum**, a less likely interpretation would be "in one victory.")

Campānī seems to refer to the inhabitants of one of the wards in Pompeii and not to those of the region of Campania.

p. 114 Dead gladiator from fourth-century mosaic of gladiatorial combats, from Torre Nuova. His name, Aureus, is given on the mosaic though not in this detail (*Rome, Borghese Gallery*).

Suggestions for further activities

Imaginative writing is a useful response to this material. Possible scenarios include:

1 You have taken a blind friend to the amphitheater for the afternoon. Describe what is happening.

2 Two gladiators are waiting in the tunnel just before going out into the arena to fight. They have trained together and are personal friends. What might they say to each other?

3 This pottery fragment in the Jewry Wall Museum, Leicester, England, is scratched with the graffito **Verecunda [et] ludia Lucius gladiator**, linking the name of an actress with that of a gladiator. What might the actress say to her gladiator to dissuade him from going on fighting in the arena, now that he has been presented with his wooden sword? What reasons might he give for continuing?

4 Additional activities might include: designing posters; creating a diorama; producing a radio program with recorded commentary and discussions; or a newspaper report of a fight.

5 Show a clip from *A.D.*, *Barabbas*, *Gladiator*, *Spartacus*, or *Pompeii*. Each has exciting scenes illustrating the training programs and gladiatorial shows.

Vocabulary checklist (p. 114)

If students themselves do not notice, indicate that **gladius**, or *sword*, is related to **gladiātor**. Despite the etymology of their name, did all gladiators fight with swords?

In 1681, King Charles II of England granted a large tract of land to William Penn, to be governed on the Quaker principles that Penn had adopted. That land is now known as Penn's Woods or Pennsylvania (Penn + **silva**).

The word "sanguine" originally referred to the ruddy complexion caused when blood (**sanguis**) dominated over the other "humors." The energetic, hopeful nature of many ruddy-complexioned individuals has led to its more recent meaning.

statim shortened to "stat" is a term used in medicine to indicate that something should be done immediately.

STAGE 9: thermae

Cultural context
The Roman baths.

Story line
Quintus celebrates his birthday by a visit to the baths. He tries out his new discus with disastrous results. Metella and Melissa shop for a new toga as a present. A toga thief is caught in the baths.

Main language features
- dative singular and plural
  e.g. *mercātor fēminīs togās ostendit.*

Sentence patterns
NOM + DAT + ACC + V
e.g. *Quīntus servō pecūniam dedit.*
personal pronouns as subjects gradually suppressed
e.g. *quid quaeris, domina?*

Focus of exercises
1 Selection of verb according to sense.
2 Agreement of verb with a nominative singular or plural.
3 Completion of sentence with suitable noun or phrase, based on **in tabernā**.
All exercises practice the dative singular and plural.

Opening page (p. 115)

Illustration. Centerpiece of entrance hall of baths, surrounded by two tiers of arches and dramatically lit by a skylight above. The marble bust of Apollo incorporated a jet of water that played into the circular basin in front of it (*Suburban Baths, Herculaneum*).

Model sentences (pp. 116–117)

New language feature. The dative case (singular and plural) is introduced within the basic sentence, after the nominative, i.e. NOM + DAT + ACC + V.

New vocabulary. ad thermās, discum novum, ferēbat, statuam, nāsum frāctum, dōnum, ēlēgit, offerēbat.

First reading. Although dative forms now appear for the first time, students will probably find little difficulty, especially if you encourage them to deduce the meaning of the Latin from the illustrations. The sentences are carefully constructed to elicit the proper translation. Leading questions such as "To whom did Quintus give the money?" and "For whom were Metella and Melissa shopping?" can also be used to help students feel comfortable with this new feature.

Consolidation. Reread at the start of subsequent lessons the particular sentences which relate to the coming story.

Illustrations

p. 116 The building in the background to these line drawings combines elements from various baths in Pompeii and Herculaneum.

p. 117 The original of the amphora rack in model sentence 10 is on p. 75; a very similar lantern appears on p. 178.

in palaestrā (pp. 118–119)

Story. Caecilius takes Quintus to the baths where he meets a famous athlete and, in trying out his new discus, offends him by chipping his statue.

Consolidation. In discussing students' answers to the questions, there are opportunities:

1   To practice the perfect and imperfect tense in the way suggested on p. 54 of this manual.

2   To encourage the students to explore more deeply the motivation of the characters involved, e.g.:

> Why did Quintus break the statue? Was he nervous? careless? showing off in front of his friends?
>
> Why did the bystanders laugh at the accident? Why did Quintus laugh?
>
> Why did Milo not laugh?

3   To help students appreciate the Roman concept of honor, for oneself and the community, by exploring the attitudes shown to and by Milo, e.g.:

> Do the students regard him as arrogant? Would his contemporaries?
>
> Under what circumstances might the statue have been erected? Had he won a deciding event in an athletics match against Nuceria? Had he won a victory in Rome, bringing honor to his home town?
>
> Do modern athletes enjoy the same importance and status?

Illustration

p. 119   Palaestra of Stabian Baths, Pompeii. These baths originated before the Roman colony was established in the early first century BC and have a large exercise ground built in the days when the city's culture was more Greek than Roman.

About the language (pp. 120–121)

New language feature. Dative singular and plural.

Discussion. This is a long note, and teachers may wish to deal with paragraph 5 in a separate lesson. Start by displaying this pair of model sentences, with their translations, on the board:

> **multī hospitēs cum Quīntō cēnābant.**
> **Clēmēns hospitibus vīnum offerēbat.**

Teacher: The guests appear in both sentences, but there is a difference in the ways in which the word appears in the Latin. Can you point out the difference?

Answer: In one it is **hospitēs**, in the other **hospitibus**.

Teacher: Good. Look again at the sentence **Clēmēns hospitibus vīnum offerēbat** and notice how it is translated.

Then put up other sentences with datives (including endings in **-ae, -ō, -ī, -īs,** and **-ibus**) and invite comment. Work toward students recognizing the **-ae, -ō,** and **-ī** endings as singular and **-īs** and **-ibus** as plural, and their representation in English as "to" or "for," expressed or understood.

Consolidation. Ask the students to pick out sentences containing a dative from stories they have already read, and have the sentences translated, to remind them of the function of the dative. Do not, at this stage, expect students to cope with the dative in isolation.

in tabernā (p. 122)

Story. Metella goes shopping to buy Quintus a new toga as a birthday present. When her choice proves expensive, Melissa drives down the price.

First reading. Keep a tally on the board of Marcellus' demands and Melissa's offers.

Consolidation. After the reading is complete, discuss some of the issues which emerge, e.g.:

> Who makes the decision to buy the toga?
> Why does Melissa do all the bargaining?
> Where do people bargain like this today?

Further information. Since Quintus is celebrating his birthday, students may ask about the Roman customs. Birthdays were usually celebrated as festivals of the **genius** or guardian spirit which was believed to come into the world with a child at birth. There were offerings of wine, flowers, incense, and cakes. Friends and family gave presents to the person having the birthday. The festival usually ended with a dinner party.

Illustration. Relief of a fabric shop. Two seated customers are attended by a slave. The merchant in the center and his two assistants (who may also be slaves) display the fabric. Shutters beside the windows and roof tiles can be seen along the top (*Florence, Uffizi*).

Practicing the language (p. 123)

Exercise 1. Selection of verb for sense. Practice with the dative.

Exercise 2. Agreement of verb in the perfect with a nominative singular or plural. Practice with the dative.

Exercise 3. Completion exercise based on **in tabernā**.

Language information: revision

In Stage 7 students learnt how verbs are listed in the Vocabulary. Now is a good time to do the same for nouns. The explanation and practice examples are set out on p. 191, paragraphs 1–3. Further examples could be taken from recent stories and Vocabulary checklists.

**in apodytēriō (p. 124)

Play. Two attendants in the apodyterium apprehend a man stealing a toga.

First reading. The story is harder than it looks because it contains most of the nouns, verb endings, and sentence patterns introduced so far.

Further information. Pleading mitigating circumstances and appealing to the pity of the judges were a regular feature of defense in Roman courts.

Illustrations

p. 124 Mosaic of squid in women's changing room (*Central Baths, Herculaneum*). Marine motifs were popular for baths (see also the octopus on p. 130), and the simplicity of black and white, rather than colored, mosaic often produced a crisp and vivid effect.

p. 125 • Women's changing room (*Stabian Baths, Pompeii*), with barrel-vaulted ceiling, benches around three sides, and recesses for clothing. Behind the photographer is a small cold-water tank; unlike the men, Pompeian women did not have a separate frigidarium.
  • Reconstruction of men's caldarium (*Forum Baths, Pompeii*).

Cultural context material (pp. 126–129)

Content. The text and picture essay describe a visit to the baths. The different rooms, activities, and heating system are explored in some detail.

Suggestions for discussion. One way of approaching the information is to start with the picture essay, and encourage students to support their own observations by referring to the text. The technical terms for the different areas of the baths can be hard for some students to remember. A lively, if somewhat noisy, activity for younger students to help with this is to label different areas of the classroom and have the students visit the different rooms and enact what took place in them.

Further information. Some details in the students' material are particular to the baths in Pompeii, and some are general features.

Baths were a popular and fashionable meeting place in Roman life, providing both public hygiene and a lively social center. Critics saw them as an indication of social decadence like extravagant dinner parties; some were a cover for prostitution. But the majority contributed to general social well-being and to public hygiene (although without chlorine and constant changes of the water, one must question how hygienic the baths really were). The uninhibited delight of the Pompeians in the pleasures of bathing, the chatter of friends, and the shouts of attendants and peddlers must have filled these barrel-vaulted rooms with an echoing din and much happy excitement. Help the students imagine the noise and variety of activities by comparing Roman baths with crowded indoor pools, a PE complex, health clubs, or the Y.

The main hours of bathing were in the afternoon. Sometimes women (and elderly people) went in the morning to baths which did not have separate provision, and sometimes there was mixed bathing. Most baths were run as commercial enterprises by individuals who leased them for a period of time. The contractor (**conductor**) appointed a superintendent (**balneātor**) and charged a small entrance fee. Bathers, or their slaves, brought with them their own olive oil, strigils, and personal toiletry sets (nail cleaner, tweezers, earscoop, etc.).

Use a ruler to demonstrate the use of a strigil. Metal strigils are still used in the grooming of horses, and wooden strigils were used by Native Americans.

In Pompeii there were numerous baths of different sizes. For instance, the House of Julia Felix contains a small set of baths which was open to the public. The main large baths were:

1   The Forum Baths, built about 80 BC. They have separate sections for men and women.
2   The Stabian Baths, at the junction of Via di Stabia and Via dell' Abbondanza. The oldest, dating from the second century BC, they were constantly updated. In their final form they were lavishly equipped and decorated, having some of the finest stucco decoration that still survives. They had separate sections for men and women.
3   The Suburban Baths, just outside the Marine Gate.

4 The Central Baths, at the junction of Via di Stabia and Via di Nola. These were started as part of the public works program after the earthquake of AD 62 or 63, but were never finished. The design was grand, with large, airy, well-lit rooms.

Illustrations

p. 126 Bathers would carry a set of strigils with differing curvatures and a small flask of oil (*Naples, Archaeological Museum*).

p. 127 Picture essay, suggesting bather's route around the baths:
    (1)   Rich stucco decoration in men's Stabian Baths, Pompeii.
    (2)   The **tepidārium** of the men's Forum Baths, Pompeii. A brazier with bronze benches grouped around it can be seen at the rear behind a modern grille. Heating the warm room by brazier instead of underfloor heating was an outdated method by AD 79, but was still in operation at the Forum Baths while the Stabian Baths were out of use for renovation.
    (3, 4) Women's Central Baths, Herculaneum. The grooved ceiling in (3) channeled condensation down the walls.
    (5)   Men's Forum Baths, Pompeii.

p. 128 Bronze boxer, found on the site of the Baths of Constantine, Rome. He has a scarred face with blood oozing from cuts. He wears the Roman form of boxing gloves (leather strips reinforced with lead) and arm bands to wipe sweat and blood out of his eyes (*Rome, Museo Nazionale Romano*).

p. 129 ● Hypocaust in men's Stabian Baths (pictured on p. 119) where the hot air circulated under the floor and rose up inside double walls with built-in spacers. The arched hole behind the water tank (towards top right of photograph) would have led to a half-cylindrical tank with its flat side supported above a small fire to keep the water hot.
    ● Plan of Forum Baths, Pompeii, with light blue representing water (bathing tanks and boilers). It is not quite accurate on the men's side, where an old-fashioned brazier was being used (see note to p. 127), but reflects what became standard Roman practice.

p. 130 Octopus, Women's Central Baths, Herculaneum (cf. p. 124).

Suggestions for further activities

1 Design and label, perhaps on computer, the ground plan for a Roman bathing complex.
2 Imagine you are an attendant at a Roman bath and that you are describing your job to a friend, while having a drink with him or her in the evening at an inn.
3 Research Roman birthday customs and, especially, the coming of age customs.

Vocabulary checklist (p. 130)

"Agnostic" (from **agnoscit**) should mean "recognizing," not its opposite. The word was actually coined by T.H. Huxley in the nineteenth century, based on the Greek prefix *a* meaning "not," combined with *gnostic* (Greek for "knowing").

    dat gives us "dative," the Latin case used for indirect objects, to whom something is "given, offered, told, shown."

    post gives us "postscript," "postpone," and "postpositive" among others.

STAGE 10: rhētor

Cultural context
The Roman education system; books and writing materials.

Story line
At the rhetor's, Quintus and his Greek friend, Alexander, debate the respective merits of the Romans and the Greeks. Quintus resolves a quarrel between Alexander's two young brothers. Grumio finds a magic ring in the street. Lucia talks to Melissa about Alexander.

Main language features
- 1st and 2nd persons plural present (including **sum**)
  e.g. *nōs Graecī sumus sculptōrēs. vōs Rōmānī estis barbarī.*
- comparative adjectives
  e.g. *nōs sumus callidiōrēs quam vōs.*

Sentence patterns
NOM + DAT et DAT + ACC + V
e.g. *Quīntus rhētorī et amīcīs argūmentum explicāvit.*
est in the final position
e.g. *ānulus antīquus est.*

Focus of exercises
1 1st person plural of present.
2 Nominative complements in 1st and 2nd person plural sentences.

Opening page (p. 131)

Illustration. Marble statue of an elderly Greek teaching. The students might like to look at his hand and suggest what he is saying, e.g. "Listen to this," or "There are four points," or **nōs Graecī Rōmānōs docēmus** (p. 135). He is, in fact, the philosopher Chrysippus (*c.* 280–207 BC), a prominent member of the Stoic school of philosophers, whose teachings were studied and followed by many educated Romans. He is included here as a symbol of the important part that Greeks played in Roman education. The statue is now in the Louvre in Paris, though the head is a cast of one in the British Museum in London (*photograph by Giraudon*).

Model sentences (pp. 132–135)

New language feature. 1st and 2nd person plural of the present (including **sum**).

New vocabulary. nōs, sumus, architectī, pontēs, aedificāmus, fundōs, sculptōrēs, pictōrēs, vōs, estis, barbarī, ūtilēs, quam (*than*), **docēmus.**

First reading. Set the scene of a debate, using students as debaters, and make clear that:
1 One speaker puts forward the Roman claims, while the other advances the Greek case.
2 The task of the class is to discover the claims and criticisms made on each side.
   Students with a knowledge of Spanish, French, or Italian have little difficulty with **nōs** and **vōs**; for others the introductory sentences (**Rōmānus dīcit/Graecus dīcit**) provide the clue.

Illustrations. The pictures contain a good deal of detail and it is helpful to discuss each picture for a few moments before tackling the caption:

1 Surveying along a road for a public building, using a **grōma** and poles. A surveyor would plant the stake of the **grōma** firmly in the ground, check by the plumb lines that it was absolutely upright, and look along the arms to mark out a straight line or along the cords to mark out a right angle.

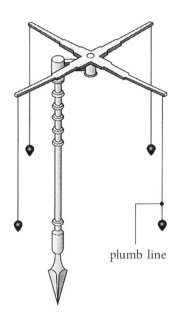

plumb line

2 Country estate with pigs and cattle. Note the terracing and the plow drawn by oxen wearing a yoke.

3 Making a copy of a Greek marble statue. The apparatus at the right would have been used to measure the height at key points of the statue to ensure that the copy was accurate. You might also ask if anyone recognizes the famous statue that the Greek craftsmen are copying. It is, in fact, the Doryphoros, or "Spear-bearer," originally by Polykleitos, a fifth-century BC Greek sculptor. The most perfect copy yet found of this statue came from the Samnite Palaestra at Pompeii. There is a Roman copy of this statue in the Minneapolis Art Museum.

4 Painting murals. The wall was prepared with three coats of fine polished plaster. The painting was done while the surface was still wet, so that the colors were absorbed into the plaster. The paints were made from powdered minerals mixed with egg or honey, made up as required.

5 Greek engrossed in a play, while his fellows sleep.

6 Roman legionaries fighting barbarians. The Romans are wearing helmets designed to protect their necks, cheeks, and noses, and body armor made of strips of metal. They carry rectangular shields and swords. Note their disciplined formation and their efficient sword technique in contrast with that of the barbarians.

7 Installing a public toilet: putting in stone seating at back, adjusting a tap at front. Note the lack of privacy.

8 Teacher and class.

Consolidation. The sentences draw a contrast between Greek intellectual and artistic skills and Roman practicality. Draw this out in discussion by asking the students what difference they notice in the *kind* of things the two nations are proud of.

controversia (pp. 136–137)

Story. The rhetor sets as a debating topic "Greeks are better than Romans." Quintus and his friend Alexander take opposing sides. Quintus earns the applause of the other students but Alexander is judged by the teacher to have made the better case.

First reading. This story contains little action. Although the arguments are presented in simple and fairly concrete terms, it can go flat unless you help the class to understand:

1 The more abstract words and phrases, e.g. **nōs tamen nōn sententiam quaerimus, nōs argūmentum quaerimus** (lines 11–12) and **Graeciōrēs quam nōs Graecī** (lines 30–31).

2 The formality of an exercise intended to prepare well-to-do young men for the duties of politics and the law courts.

3   The emotional involvement of the speakers in their arguments, which express their cultural and national identity and their racial prejudices.

4   The interest in this topic in Pompeii, with its history of a mixed Greek and Roman population. Note that the teacher would have been a Greek himself, perhaps a freedman.

Some possible questions are:

> Why did the class applaud Quintus?
>
> Why was it Alexander who replied to Quintus?
>
> At line 31 (before reading the rest of the story): Who do you think should win the debate? Why?
>
> Do you agree with Theodorus' verdict? Could he be accused of bias?

Consolidation. In discussion, some of the historical and cultural references in the two speeches may be explained, and the examples considered. The examples given by Quintus and Alexander follow the argument in the model sentences and are further illustrated by the photographs on p. 137: the Romans are the practical ones, the Greeks the men of ideas. Discuss whether this is oversimplified.

Have students also notice the tripartite debating technique Quintus uses, by summarizing the three arguments he develops. Then have them analyze Alexander's emotional, witty rebuttal. Encourage students to use their textbooks; the value of the discussion lies in the review of Latin meanings that it encourages.

Note the student in the picture dressed in red and green: this is Alexander, with his clothes colored to match the video version of **contrōversia**.

Students may enjoy their own debate on the subject. Divide the class into Greeks and Romans and ask them to put forward their cases based on the story and the model sentences.

Illustrations

p. 137 ● The bridge at Alcantara (*c.* AD 106), considered the finest bridge in the Roman world. It is almost 173 yards (200 meters) long, and the arches rise nearly 55 yards (50 meters) above the river Tagus. It is constructed in stone, without mortar, and designed to withstand violent flooding of the river. Roman architecture is famous for the skillful use of arches in bridges, aqueducts, and buildings such as the Colosseum.

● Marble portrait of Euripides (485?–406? BC). The head looks rather too small because the statue is actually a composite; a head of Euripides is attached to the body of an unidentified dramatist holding a tragic mask (*Rome, Vatican Museums*).

● Mosaic of Anaximander of Miletus, born 610 BC (*Trier, Rheinisches Landesmuseum*).

About the language 1 (p. 138)

New language feature. 1st and 2nd person plural. All persons of the present tense (including **sum**) have now been met and are tabulated here.

Discussion. Begin by asking the students what they have noticed in the model sentences. Most will mention **nōs** and **vōs**; some will have spotted the new verb endings. See what progress they make with the formulation of rules; then proceed with the language note.

Depending on the confidence shown by the students, you may find it necessary to tackle the note in three parts: paragraphs 1–2, 3–4, and 5. If this is the case, it is sensible to postpone 3–4 until **statuae** has been read, since it contains more examples of the 1st and 2nd person plural with the pronoun omitted.

Consolidation. Practice orally 1st and 2nd person plural of common verbs, initially with **nōs** and **vōs**, then dropping the pronouns. Then practice the whole of the present tense, again phasing the pronouns out gradually.

statuae (p. 139)

Story. Quintus goes home with Alexander, who on the way buys some statuettes as birthday presents for his young brothers. As they quarrel over who should receive which statuette, Quintus demonstrates Roman peacemaking skills by allocating to each brother the statuette suited to his disposition, and keeping one for himself.

First reading. Take the passage at a brisk pace, bringing out the contrast between the petulance of the small boys and the comparative maturity of the others. Many students will admit to similar experiences with young siblings.

Consolidation. Ask the students to pick out examples of the 1st and 2nd person plural. Discuss examples where the pronouns are omitted (lines 24 and 34). If you have not already done so, read paragraphs 3–4 of About the language 1, p. 138.

Illustration. Three small terracotta statuettes (*Taranto, Museo Nazionale Archeologico*).

About the language 2 (p. 140)

New language feature. The comparative adjective. The superlative degree was explained in Stage 8. This note should present no difficulties, as the comparative has become familiar from the arguments in this Stage, but make a point of discussing the difference between singular and plural forms.

Consolidation. Students enjoy going back through the stories in the Course to see how many examples they can find.

**ānulus Aegyptius (pp. 140–141)

Story. An antique Egyptian ring stolen from a pyramid brings ill luck to those who receive it, and ends up with Grumio and Poppaea.

First reading. With more-able students, try breaking off your reading in Latin to ask the class who has the ring at each particular moment. They enjoy working out the answer, and it is a good aural comprehension exercise.

Note that from now on **est** is also found in the final position, e.g. **ānulus antīquus est**.

The passage contains a range of language features including: shifts between present and past time, perfect and imperfect tenses, **quod** and **postquam** clauses, and many examples of the dative case. Give the students enough time and help with the first reading to ensure that they can attempt the comprehension questions successfully.

Illustration. Bronze ring, decorated with heads of the Egyptian gods, Isis and Serapis (*London, British Museum*). Care has been taken not to show a gold ring, as at this time the wearing of gold rings was restricted by law to senators and members of the order of Roman knights (**equitēs**). If Grumio had been found wearing one, it would definitely not have been his lucky day.

Lūcia et Alexander (p. 142)

Play. Lucia and Melissa walk near the palaestra and see Alexander. The girls discuss the relative merits of two boys: Alexander and Quintus.

First reading. This is a short play to round off the Stage and should not provide the students with many difficulties. A dramatic reading by the teacher may be all that is needed to give the students a strong grasp of how the conversation develops.

Consolidation. The play provides a good opportunity to review comparatives and superlatives, as well as two uses of **quam**. In lines 8 and 15, **quam** is used with an adjective to express exclamation, e.g. **quam pulcher est Alexander!** *How beautiful is Alexander!* In lines 12–13, **quam** is used with a comparative adjective, meaning "than," e.g. **Alexander est callidior quam Quīntus.** *Alexander is cleverer than Quintus.*

Students should also be encouraged to consider what the play tells us about the relationship between Lucia and Melissa, and about Lucia's attitude toward other civilizations.

Practicing the language (p. 142)

Exercise 1. Completing sentence with verb in 1st person plural according to sense. You may need to discuss the meaning of the phrases in the tinted box before the students write their answers.

Exercise 2. Completing sentence containing **sumus** or **estis** with an appropriate nominative according to sense.

Language information

With the introduction of the dative in Stage 9, students have met all the cases of the noun presented in Unit 1. This is a good time to review the noun tables and the uses of the cases set out on p. 182 and to work through the exercises on p. 183.

Cultural context material (pp. 143–145)

Content. An outline of the Roman education system, and the preparation it gave for adult life.

Suggestions for discussion. Take the material in two stages: the earliest phase of education, and the tools for reading and writing; then the skills developed in the later phases, and the activities in public life for which they were a preparation.

Discussion might focus on the differences and similarities between Roman and modern education, including the purpose of education.

Illustrations

p. 143 • Line drawings of writing materials. See also the information given on p. 42 of this manual.

• A well-preserved wax tablet of the second century AD. The line the schoolboy has had to write out is from the poet Menander: "Accept advice from a wise man. Let no one trust in his friends rashly." This is an appropriate copybook precept. Notice the ruled lines as a guide for the pupil (*London, British Library, Add. MS 341187(1)II*).

p. 144 • A stone relief showing a school scene (third century AD, from Neumagen, Germany). The teacher is shown bearded in the Greek manner; he has a footstool. Two pupils sit in high-backed chairs while a third seems to be arriving late, carrying a bag which would contain his tablets, **stilus**, and so on (*Trier, Rheinisches Landesmuseum*).

• A poorly preserved painting from the series of forum scenes in the House of Julia Felix at Pompeii (cf. pp. 48-49; also note on p. 44 of this manual). We can make out the forum colonnade with its garlands hanging between the columns. Pupils (one barely visible) sit at left while a schoolmaster (right) flogs a boy who is supported on the back of another student. The standing figures (center left) could be bystanders in the forum (*Naples, Archaeological Museum*).

p. 145 • In this third-century AD mosaic, Virgil is seen composing the *Aeneid*, flanked by Clio, the muse of history (left) and Melpomene, the muse of tragedy (*Tunis, Bardo Museum*).

• Carving a table leg: marble relief, detail from third-century AD sarcophagus (*Rome, Vatican Museums*).

p. 146 Writing materials: detail from Pompeian wall painting. The title label can be seen hanging from the papyrus roll, and a dot in the center of the open pages of the wax tablet represents a raised stud sometimes left in the middle of a page to prevent the two wax surfaces rubbing against each other when the tablet was closed (*Naples, Archaeological Museum*).

Suggestions for further activities

1 Write a report card for Quintus (or a younger girl or boy in Pompeii).
2 If there is time, students may enjoy learning the Greek alphabet and transliterating some Greek and English words.

Vocabulary checklist (p. 146)

callidus means *clever*, while **calidus** means *hot*. A **caldārium** is a hot room, not a clever room.

Compare **nōs**, **vōs** to the Spanish *nosotros, vosotros* and the French *nous, vous*.

Students may wonder about the connection of "importune" with **portus**. Just as "opportune" means "pressing toward the harbor," so the verb "importune" has a similar sense of urging on to a destination or desire.

semper offers an opportunity to introduce common Latin mottoes such as **semper fidēlis** and **semper parātus**. Students may remember **servat**, or *saves*, incorrectly as *serves*, **servit**. If necessary, you should teach them a mnemonic device, like **servat** and *saves* both contain the letter "a."

STAGE 11: candidātī

Cultural context
Pompeii: elections and local government.

Story line
Quintus and Lucia support different candidates in the election and make use of the services of a signwriter. Grumio finds a way of taking part in the elections, at some cost to himself. Lucia reveals her true feelings for Alexander and narrowly avoids marriage.

Main language features
- intransitive verbs with dative
  e.g. *nōs mercātōrī favēmus.*
- **placet**
  e.g. *mihi placet.*
- **nōs, vōs**: nominative, dative, and accusative
  e.g. *deī nōbīs imperium dant.*

- different ways of asking questions:
  quis, quid, etc.
  no interrogative
  -ne
  num
  e.g. *quō festīnās, Grumiō? num tū Āfrō favēs?*

Sentence patterns
NOM + DAT + V
e.g. *nōs candidātō nostrō nōn crēdimus sed favēmus.*

Focus of exercises
1 Selection of verb in correct person.
2 Selection of noun in correct case.

Opening page (p. 147)

Illustration. Marble statue from the junction of the Via dell' Abbondanza and the Via di Stabia showing the most famous of the Holconii, Marcus Holconius Rufus, in military dress. Somewhat earlier than the Holconius of this Stage, he held the duovirate five times at Pompeii, served in the Roman army, and had a career in Rome. He was described as **patrōnus** of the city of Pompeii, and paid for improvements to the temple of Apollo and the large theater (*Naples, Archaeological Museum*).

Model sentences (pp. 148–149)

New language feature. A new sentence pattern NOM + DAT + V, in which the dative is used in the following two ways:
1 With **faveō** and **crēdō**, e.g. **nōs Lūciō favēmus**.
2 With a verb of replying, e.g. **mercātōrēs agricolīs respondent**.

New vocabulary. candidātōs, noster, favēmus, crēdimus.

First reading. Guide students through their first encounters with **favēmus** and **crēdimus** with carefully crafted questions which will help them to expect a dative in association with these verbs. Then move to a more natural translation. An approach to model sentence 2, for example, may be as follows:

> Teacher: Who are shouting?
> Students: The farmers.
> Teacher: Good. What are we farmers shouting? *or* What do we have?
> Students: We have the best candidate.

Teacher:	Good. What is the name of our candidate?
Students:	Lucius.
Teacher:	Good. So in the final sentence, who do we say we give our support to?
Students:	Lucius.
Teacher:	Good. So how would we translate **nōs Lūciō favēmus**?
Students:	We give our support to Lucius.
Teacher:	Good. How might we say that more naturally or simply in English?
Students:	We support Lucius.

A similar approach can be adopted in sentences 4, 5, and 6, initially representing **crēdimus** as "we give our trust" before moving to "we trust."

Discussion. Although women could not vote in elections, their interest and investment in the politics are obvious from the graffiti found on the walls of Pompeii: of the slogans from the final seventeen years of the town's existence in which a rogator is named, approximately 7 percent were sponsored or co-sponsored by women. Therefore a number of women are pictured among the supporters of the electoral candidates.

Perceptive students may discern a difference between the bright white togas worn by the electoral candidates and the rather dirty togas sported by Roman men elsewhere in Unit 1. Students may enjoy discussing why the athlete has chosen not to wear his toga and also considering the idea of thieves having their own candidate, but not trusting him. Discussion may then lead to situations in the modern world where people group together to advance their interests, perhaps not always trusting one another.

Quīntus et Lūcia (p. 150)

Story. Lucia and Quintus are arguing about the best candidate: Lucia supports Afer, a wealthy and intelligent property owner; Quintus prefers Holconius because he is of noble birth and the Caecilii have traditionally supported the Holconii. Quintus pays a signwriter ten denarii to paint a slogan on the house wall in support of Holconius.

First reading. This story and the next should be planned together. Study the first five paragraphs of the cultural context note (p. 159) as a preliminary to the stories to give the students a realistic context for their reading. Introduce suspense at the end of this story by emphasizing in your Latin reading **mihi** in line 22, and invite students to suggest the sequel.

mihi placet and **tibi placet** are introduced with the dative in first position. Encourage a range of natural English translations, e.g. for **placetne tibi?**: "Does that suit you?" or "Is that okay for you?"

Consolidation. Oral practice of the new language features in the story is useful preparation for the next story. Alternatively, discuss About the language 1 paragraphs 1–5, if students are dealing confidently with **faveō** and **crēdō**.

Sulla (p. 151)

Story. Lucia makes the signwriter wipe out the pro-Holconius slogan and pays him to replace it with one supporting Afer. When Quintus objects, Sulla paints two signs, pleasing both Lucia and Quintus and earning thirty denarii.

First reading. Possible questions might be:

Why was Lucia angry (line 2)?

Was the slogan completely true (lines 10–11)?

Why did Lucia want the words **et frāter** included?

How much money did Sulla make from Lucia and Quintus altogether (line 27)?

Note. There is no concrete evidence that a girl like Lucia either did or did not have access to money to pay Sulla the signwriter.

Consolidation. The two stories are good for dramatic reading in Latin. Having the actors exaggerate the imperatives and superlatives will help create the enthusiastic political atmosphere. Have the student-scriptor write his or her **titulī** on the board with colored chalk.

About the language 1 (p. 152)

New language features. **faveō**, etc. with dative; dative with the impersonal **placet**; and the dative form of **nōs** and **vōs**.

Discussion. If paragraphs 1–5 were studied after **Quīntus et Lūcia**, a few fresh examples should give sufficient practice.

Consolidation. Ask the students to pick out examples of **placet** in the two stories and to work out the most appropriate English translation according to the moment in the story and the person speaking.

**Lūcius Spurius Pompōniānus (pp. 153–155)

These four scenes of boisterous comedy give review practice with the present tense and with the dative and accusative cases, while appealing to the classroom actors. The scenes should all be given a first reading at a brisk pace. If time is short, the class could then be divided into four groups, each responsible for acting a scene.

**in vīllā (p. 153)

Play. Grumio sets off to the election in the guise of a Roman citizen. Clemens goes with him because he is worried about the risk Grumio is taking.

First reading. Some useful questions for the first reading of this scene:

Why does Clemens think that Grumio ought to support Holconius?

Why does Grumio support Afer?

Why does Grumio give himself three names? (You may wish to suggest also that his full name comes close to meaning "Lucius, the phony Pompeian.")

Why does Clemens describe Grumio's plan as **perīculōsam** (line 22)?

Why is it appropriate, if illegal, for Grumio to support the bakers' candidate? (You may wish to add the suggestion that, as a cook, he would have an easier time inventing a "cover story" for his new-found citizen occupation.)

Illustration. This electoral notice reads:

CN HELVIVM SABINVM AED D R P O V F

Gnaeum Helvium Sabinum aedilem dignum re publica oramus vos faciatis.

We beg you to make Cnaeus Helvius Sabinus aedile. He is worthy of public office.

prope amphitheātrum (p. 154)

Play. Grumio is pleased to be given five denarii by Afer's election agent, but disconcerted to be handed a club.

First reading. Some useful questions:

> On which word of Grumio's speech, **salvē ... sumus** (lines 4–6) does he thump Clemens?
> Why does Grumio describe himself and Afer as **amīcissimī**?
> What does Grumio receive in addition to the denarii? Why?

in forō (pp. 154–155)

Play. Grumio and Clemens join the bakers who are accompanying Afer to the forum. They are perturbed to spot Caecilius with Holconius, and Grumio flees. A fight breaks out between the parties.

First reading. Questions could include:

> How does Grumio's tone of voice change during his speech, **euge! ... ad vīllam reveniō!** (lines 7–9)?
> Suggest why Caecilius was a supporter of Holconius.

Consolidation. Ask students to pick out and translate the comparatives and the superlative in the story: **melior** (lines 3 and 13); **fortiōrēs** (line 24); **fortissimī** (line 21).

Illustration. The photograph shows the speaker's platform (**tribūnal**) located near the middle of the west side of the forum. In the background on the left is the colonnade fronting Eumachia's building.

in culīnā (p. 155)

Story. Grumio tells Clemens he was mistaken for a baker because of the club, beaten up by the opposition, and relieved of the five denarii. Clemens displays the ten denarii given him for rescuing Caecilius from the fight, and goes off to meet Poppaea at the harbor.

First reading. Some useful questions:

1 In what state is Grumio's toga now? What state was it in at the start of the play? How do you know?
2 Why did the merchants describe Grumio as **fortis** (line 5) when they saw him in the forum?
3 Where had Grumio obtained the denarii that the merchants seized from him?
4 In what way has Poppaea apparently changed her affections? Suggest a reason.
5 Do you feel sorry for Grumio at the end of the play? Or do you feel he deserved what he got?

Note. When the students have completed their work on these scenes, ask them to predict the result of the election. They may be interested to know that in the elections to the duovirate in Pompeii in AD 79, the victorious candidates were M. Holconius Priscus and C. Cerrinus Vatia.

About the language 2 (p. 156)

New language feature. Questions.

Discussion. As the note summarizes the types of questions met so far, there should be no problems. **num** should be treated as a vocabulary item *surely … not?* when encountered in stories and not discussed further unless students ask. **nōnne** is introduced in Unit 2.

Consolidation. Repeated spells of five-minute oral practice of the questioning words and question spotting in future stories are both useful. Ask students to reply (in Latin, if possible) to simple oral questions in Latin, e.g. **quis es? ubi habitās?**

Practicing the language (p. 157)

Exercise 1. Selection of verb in correct person.

Exercise 2. Selection of noun in correct case or number (examples are restricted to nominative and accusative). Point out that two language points are practiced here.

Language information

This can be a good point in the Course to study p. 189 "Word order" and p. 190 "Longer sentences with **postquam** and **quod.**"

Lūcia et Metella (p. 158)

Play. Metella explains to Lucia that her father has chosen a husband for her: a rather elderly man named Umbricius. Tears ensue as Lucia explains she loves Alexander. Lucia has a lucky escape when Umbricius instead marries one of his ex-slaves. She thanks the gods for saving her.

First reading. The first sentence of Metella's speech is likely to come as quite a shock to the students. Once it is understood, students are likely to want to read the rest of the play quickly, in order to find out what happens. Use oral comprehension questions to generate pace, e.g.

> Why did Caecilius write to Holconius?
> In line 5, how does Holconius describe his friend?
> What happened to Umbricius' last wife?
> How do you think she might have died?

Consolidation. This is a good opportunity to discuss the relationship between Metella and Lucia. Students may be encouraged to consider why it is that Caecilius arranges the marriage, but Metella breaks the news to Lucia. What is the tone of Metella's speech? Is Lucia closer to her mother or her father? What does the passage tell us about marriage in the Roman world, and about a master's possible reasons for freeing a slave girl? For further consolidation, students may wish to act out the play in small groups.

Cultural context material (pp. 159–161)

Content. The system of local government and the way in which Roman values of public service influenced small-town life. The material divides into three sections: general introduction (p. 159 paras 1–5); the tradition of public service (p. 159 para. 6 and p. 160); and election notices (pp. 160–161).

Suggestions for discussion. Read the general introduction (p. 159) before embarking on the stories and discuss the other sections at convenient points. Invite students to comment on the process of electioneering described in this Stage. Help them see similarities and differences with local politics in their own town. (Who are the local officials? How often are they elected? How do the candidates gather support? What does a member of the town council do? What does the mayor or town manager do?) You might want to discuss the direct and indirect forms of bribery practiced by Roman politicians. Discuss the significance of the Latin tag: **pānem et circēnsēs** (Juvenal, *Satire* X, 79).

Further information

Local Government. Local government in Pompeii was based on elective officers. The bureaucracy of central government had not yet stifled local politics and competition was lively, especially for the post of **aedīlis**, since appointment as **duovir** followed almost automatically. A magistrate took office in July, after success at the polls in March. When the eruption occurred, the **duovirī** had been in office for about a month and the town was still plastered with electoral propaganda.

Electoral Slogans. The sponsors of a candidate usually based their appeal on character, not on political platforms, since there was little scope for differences in political policy. Various factions supported candidates as shown in the model sentences of this Stage. Other groups who supported candidates were **mūliōnēs** (mule drivers), **sāgariī** (cloak cutters), **saccāriī** (porters), **fullōnēs** (cloth makers), **piscicāpī** (fishermen), even **latrunculāriī** (chess players), and many others. Some of the graffiti appear to have been put up to discredit a candidate: the **dormientēs ūniversī** (all the sleepyheads) back the unlucky Vatia.

Election notices followed a simple formula, e.g.:

> **A Vettium Firmum aed. o.v.f. dign. est**
> (We urge you to make Aulus Vettius Firmus aedile. He is worthy.)
> (**o.v.f.** is an abbreviation of **ōrāmus vōs faciātis**.)
> **Caprasia cum Nymphio rog.**
> (Caprasia asks this with Nymphius.)

Skilled signwriters put up notices that were intended to be seen, even from a distance. The letters were usually painted in red (sometimes black for gladiatorial notices; see picture on p. 161), and were often a foot (30 cm) high. Sometimes they were signed by the writers; e.g., **scripsit Protogenes** and **scr. Infantio cum Floro et Fructo et Sabino hic et ubique**. So many graffiti covered the walls that an anonymous satirist wrote:

> **admiror, paries, te non cecidisse ruinis,**
> **qui tot scriptorum taedia sustineas.**
> I am surprised, wall, that you have not collapsed in ruins since you bear the weight of the rubbish of so many hacks.

For additional graffiti see Marx.

Illustrations

p. 159 ● The westernmost of the three municipal offices (number 7 on the aerial photograph, p. 51). This was probably the **cūria** or meeting place of the decurions, who formed the local senate. At the end is an apse where the presiding officials would have sat; the recesses were probably intended for statues; and the scaffolding holes visible in the brickwork were designed to be concealed by a marble facing.

● A wall painting from Pompeii that may just show a bakery, but the toga worn by the man behind the counter makes it possible that he is an official or candidate distributing free bread to the people. The circular loaves piled on the counter are similar to the one shown on p. 24 (*Naples, Archaeological Museum*).

p. 160 ● Temple of Fortuna Augusta. The walls of the **cella** (the room housing the god's statue) survive, as do the steps leading up to them, flanking an altar in the middle. We have to imagine the row of columns that originally ran in front of the **cella** and supported the gabled roof. The wooden railing is modern.

● Front view of statue of M. Holconius Rufus (cf. p. 147).

p. 161 This illustration is based on inscriptions found on the wall of the House of Trebius Valens. Electoral graffiti in Pompeii appear mainly on the upper part of walls. But as the upper part of this wall was full of slogans, lower parts of the wall were whitewashed to allow more messages to be added. The inscriptions are (clockwise from top left):

● **lanternari tene scalam.**
Hold on to the ladder, lantern bearer.

● **Gaium Iulium Polybium aedilem viis aedibus sacris publicis procurandis.**
[Vote for] *Gaius Julius Polybius as aedile for supervising roads, temples, and public works.*

● **Decimi Lucreti Satri Valentis flaminis gladiatorum paria decem pugnabunt.**
Ten pairs of gladiators owned by Decimus Lucretius Satrius Valens, priest, will fight.

● **Quintum Postumium Modestum.**
[Vote for] *Quintus Postumius Modestus.*

● **Lucium Ceium Secundum duovirum oramus faciatis.**
We beg you to make Lucius Ceius Secundus duovir.

● **Marcum Holconium duovirum iure dicundo dignum re publica oramus vos faciatis.**
We beg you to make Marcus Holconius duovir for administering justice; he is worthy of public office.

● **Cnaeum Helvium Sabinum aedilem oramus faciatis.**
We beg you to make Gnaeus Helvius Sabinus aedile.

p. 162 Another electoral notice:

L CEIVM SECVNDVM AED ORPHAEVS FACIT

Lucium Ceium Secundum aedilem Orphaeus facit.

Orphaeus makes Lucius Ceius Secundus aedile.

Suggestions for further activities

1   Hold a mock election, using the information in the Stage to put forward candidates, slogans, graffiti, speeches, etc.
2   Help the students to decipher and interpret the graffiti on p. 161 of their textbook. They might enjoy preparing poster, PowerPoint, or website graffiti in Latin for either actual or imaginary school elections. Encourage students to use the abbreviation **o.v.f.** and model their slogans after those in their textbook.
3   Write and deliver an imaginary campaign speech, in English, by a Pompeian candidate for the aedileship in the forum. Don't forget your promises to various power groups such as the merchants and bakers. Include a few Latin sentences, if possible.

Vocabulary checklist (p. 162)

senātor is from the Latin word **senex**. Roman senators were the original "elder statesmen."

"Valor" and "valiant" are related to the verb **valet**, *is well*, *is strong*, of which **valē!**, *fare well*, is the singular imperative.

STAGE 12: Vesuvius

Cultural context
The eruption of Vesuvius, late summer or fall of AD 79; the excavation of Pompeii and Herculaneum.

Story line
While Caecilius is dining with Julius, Clemens comes to fetch him, because the household is alarmed by the eruption.

On the way home, Clemens takes refuge in the temple of Isis while searching for Metella and Lucia, who are trapped in a deserted store. Clemens arrives home to find the family missing and Caecilius dying. Caecilius frees Clemens, giving him his signet ring for Quintus. Cerberus remains to guard his dead master.

Main language features
- 1st and 2nd persons singular and plural, imperfect and perfect
  e.g. *tū sonōs audīvistī. ego tremōrēs sēnsī.*
- 1st and 2nd persons singular and plural, imperfect of **sum**
  e.g. *vōs tamen nōn erātis perterritī.*

Sentence patterns
Expansion of subordinate clause to contain DAT + ACC + V
e.g. *Caecilius, postquam Clēmentī ānulum suum trādidit, statim exspīrāvit.*

Opening page (p. 163)
Set the context by studying the picture of Vesuvius on this page, the line drawings on p. 164, and the picture essay on p. 173. Identifying the phenomena associated with recorded eruptions, e.g. rumblings, mushroom cloud, pyroclastic flow, ash, fire. Other useful points for discussion include:

1 The behavior of people seen in the picture on p. 163.
2 The physical dominance of the mountain in the streets and squares of Pompeii.
3 The distance of Pompeii from the mountain (see map, p. 174).
4 The attraction of living on the slopes of volcanic mountains (fertile soil, family tradition, etc.).

Illustration. Here people are fleeing from an eruption of Vesuvius on August 8th 1779 (engraving by Francesco Piranesi colored by Jean-Louis Desprez). The mountain was very active from 1631 until its last eruption in 1944. In this picture the remains of its old cone can be seen, with the new one glowing within it (*London, British Museum, Department of Prints and Drawings*).

Model sentences (pp. 164–165)
New language feature. 1st and 2nd person singular and plural of both past tenses. The perfect and the imperfect tenses are mostly shown side by side, as in Stage 6, with the imperfect representing a continuous situation and the perfect an event which is fully realized. Pronouns are used as markers at first and gradually withdrawn in this and later Stages.

New vocabulary. sonōs, tremōrēs, sēnsī, eram, nūbem, cinerem, flammās.

First reading. It is sometimes necessary to remind students of the minor characters they met a while ago: Syphax (Stage 3, pp. 28, 31) and Felix (Stage 6, pp. 72–73; Stage 7, p. 92); Lucrio and Poppaea (Stage 5, p. 61); Thrasymachus and Diodorus (Stage 10, p. 139). You might (depending on the literary experience of your students) want to suggest this reappearance is similar to the gathering together of characters in the denouement of a novel or play.

tremōrēs (pp. 166–167)

Story. Caecilius is discussing the eruption over dinner at Julius' house near Nuceria. To his surprise, Clemens, whom he had sent to his farm in the country, arrives from Pompeii asking for him.

First reading. Students become so concerned to find out what happens during the eruption that they are likely to set a fast pace for the first reading of all the stories in this Stage until they reach the climax. Support the faster pace by dramatic Latin reading, judicious section breaks, assistance with vocabulary, and pointed questions. Little help is usually required with the new structures.

Consolidation. The comprehension questions are suitable for group work, with students producing written answers. Discussion of the answers will provide an opportunity to explore the earlier earthquake, the religious beliefs of Caecilius and his household, and Caecilius' reaction to Clemens' disobedience of orders.

Further information. Caecilius rented a farm, the Fundus Audianus, for 6,000 sesterces, and we know from three surviving tablets that he found it difficult to pay the rent. The town of Nuceria, where Julius' villa was located, has already been featured in the stories of the riot at the Pompeian amphitheater in Stage 8. The illustration of Caecilius' **larārium** can be used to remind students of his thankfulness to the gods who saved his family from the earlier earthquake. Remind students also that a Roman **familia** was more extended than a North American family, and included slaves.

Illustrations

pp. 166–167 The reliefs were found on the lararium in Caecilius' house and show the effects of the earthquake that occurred in AD 62 or 63. Both reliefs appear to relate to his own experiences and may have been put up in gratitude for his preservation. The panel on p. 166 shows a scene that would have been visible from Caecilius' front door (from the left):
   - the water reservoir that supplied the street fountains, public baths, and some private houses;
   - the Vesuvius Gate collapsing;
   - by a stretch of city wall, a cart team of two mules fleeing in terror.
   The panel on p. 167 shows the honorific arch flanking the temple of Jupiter in the forum, the equestrian statues on either side of the temple, and the altar in front—all dramatically tipping over (cf. p. 52).

p. 167 Bronze statuette of a Lar, typically shown as a young man with billowing clothes, holding a shallow bowl for drink offerings in one hand and a drinking horn in the other. Shrines for the lares were sometimes in the kitchen, since they ensured that the family had plenty to eat and drink (*Oxford, Ashmolean Museum*).

ad urbem (p. 168)

Story. Clemens explains that he and the farm manager felt too afraid to stay on the farm. He found Quintus at home and was sent to fetch Caecilius. On his way home, Caecilius meets Holconius fleeing to the harbor, and is shocked by his lack of concern for Metella and the children.

First reading. Keep the story moving by dramatic Latin reading, and by breaking it down into sections at points where the students will want to continue, e.g.:

> **"quid vōs fēcistis?" rogāvit Iūlius** (line 6).
> **"Quīntus mē ad tē mīsit."** (line 13).
> **"cūr nōn ad portum fugitis?" rogāvit Holcōnius** (lines 19–20).

Consolidation. Stress the perfect forms of such verbs as **āmittere**, **dēlēre**, **contendere**, and **cōnspicere**.

If students are dealing confidently with the new persons of the verb, study About the language (pp. 172–173) at this point. Students will thus have a chance to become thoroughly familiar with these forms before undertaking a general review of verbs from the Language information section.

Note: There are some differences between this story and the video dramatization.

ad vīllam (p. 169)

Story. Caecilius finds Pompeii in chaos. He sends Clemens to search for Metella and Lucia while he returns home to look for Quintus. Amid the earth tremors Clemens takes shelter in the temple of Isis. Metella and Lucia become trapped in a deserted store as the tremors reduce it to ruins.

First reading. Again let the dramatic points of the narrative dictate the end of sections you select for the students to explore, e.g.:

> **... Quīntus nōs exspectat** (lines 5–6).
> **Lūcia cum magnā difficultāte spīrābat** (lines 13–14).

Be prepared to help at line 19 where **sumus** is introduced without **nōs**.

Consolidation. Possible discussion points:

> Why did Caecilius choose to send Clemens to look for Metella and Lucia, and himself return home to Quintus?
> How might Clemens' experience in the temple of Isis affect his view of the power of the goddess?
> Why did Lucia find it difficult to breathe?
> How close do students think Metella and Lucia's relationship is?

Further information. Note that in lines 9–10 Clemens takes shelter in the temple of Isis. In Unit 2, Clemens, now a **lībertus**, will establish himself as a glass seller in Alexandria and become a devotee of this goddess. (See also the note on the illustrations below.)

Illustrations

- Temple of Isis seen from its surrounding colonnade. Between the columns on the left can be glimpsed the entrance to a shrine and vaulted cellar which contained a pool of sacred water, representing the Nile.

- Bezel of a gold ring (enlarged), showing a bust of Isis, wearing a vulture headdress supporting the cow horns and disk of the Egyptian goddess Hathor, with whom she was identified in the Greco-Roman world. She was "Isis of the countless names," a nurturing, protective deity and a favorite among the Romans (*London, Victoria and Albert Museum*).

fīnis (pp. 170–171)

Story. After searching in vain for Metella and Lucia, Clemens reaches home to find it in ruins and Cerberus guarding his dying master. Caecilius orders Clemens to flee and to deliver his signet ring to Quintus, if he finds him.

First reading. Read the first four lines in Latin to establish the somber atmosphere of this final story and then invite interpretations from the whole group. The shifts in mood at line 10 (**dominum custōdiēbat**) and line 25 (**Clēmēns recūsāvit**) suggest appropriate sections for exploration.

Consolidation. Possible topics for discussion include:
    Which words depict the behavior of the volcano at this time?
    Find words which show Clemens' feelings. Does his mood change during the story?
    What is the significance of the ring (lines 28–29)?
    What do you think is the most significant word in the last two sentences?

The fate of the historical Caecilius is unknown. In our stories the ring he hands Clemens symbolizes Quintus' new role as head of the **familia**. Students may wish to speculate on what happens to the members of that household, including the loyal Cerberus. Do not give away Clemens' and Quintus' reappearance in Unit 2, should such a discussion occur. Other more tender-hearted students will let the dead quietly pass under the ash cover, not without tears.

Illustration. Some of the casts made by pouring plaster into the impressions in the ash which were left by decomposing bodies: children, adults, and a dog. The dog must have been struggling to free himself from his chain, hence his contorted position. Some of these people seem to have died quite peacefully, recalling Pliny the Younger's statement that his uncle's body, when found after the eruption, looked "more like a man asleep than dead" (*Letters* VI.16). The skeletons of others, not shown here, have been found torn apart by violent, explosive pyroclastic flows.

About the language (pp. 172–173)

New language features. 1st and 2nd person singular and plural of the imperfect and perfect tenses; paradigm of the full imperfect and perfect tenses; the imperfect of **sum**.

Discussion. Start by displaying some paired examples of imperfects and perfects based on the model sentences, e.g.:

    Syphāx servōs vēndēbat.   **frātrēs tremōrēs sēnsērunt.**
    Syphāx: "ego servōs vēndēbam."   **frātrēs: "nōs tremōrēs sēnsimus."**

Invite comments and proceed to the language note.
    Take the note in two parts, breaking off at the end of paragraph 2 to pick out examples from pp. 168–169 and study them in a familiar context. Then discuss paragraphs 3 and 4, asking the students to comment on the easy "regular" endings and those that are likely to

cause problems (generally **-ī, -istī, -istis**). Finally, see if they can manage the examples in paragraph 5 without reference to page 172.

Consolidation. Further practice could be based on examples of the 1st and 2nd person of the imperfect and perfect tenses found in the stories of this Stage, e.g.:

1 Ask students to find and translate examples from the text.
2 Vary the person of the examples found and ask students for a translation.
3 Omit the pronoun from some of these examples and ask for a translation.

Illustrations

- Detail of a painting from Pompeii of Vesuvius with trees and trellised vineyards almost to the summit. Part of a figure of Bacchus, dressed in grapes, symbolizing abundance and prosperity, can be seen at the left (*Naples, Archaeological Museum*).
- *Vesuvius in Eruption*, by J.M.W. Turner (*Yale Center for British Art, Paul Mellon Collection*).
- Steam rising inside the crater. Vesuvius is now overdue for an eruption and the crater is constantly monitored for seismic activity.
- The mountain from the sea. The coast is now entirely built up. This congested population will be vulnerable in any future eruption, and the Italian government has drawn up the plans for evacuation. The site of Herculaneum is roughly in the center of the picture, Pompeii outside it to the right.

Language information: review

The following work should be postponed until students are confident with all persons of the imperfect and perfect tenses. You may find it more useful for reviewing verbs in the early Stages of Unit 2.

pp. 184–186   Ensure that students are comfortable with the concept of verbs and person in paragraphs 1 and 2 before reviewing the three tenses in the chart in paragraph 3 and the meanings given in paragraph 4. Then study paragraph 5, which formally introduces the four conjugations. Ask students what similarities and differences they see. The exercise in paragraph 6 is easy and can be done orally, while those in paragraphs 7 and 8 are good tests of persons and tenses if worked without reference to the chart. After reviewing **sum** and **eram** in paragraph 9, give students written and oral practice with their books closed.

pp. 187–188   Paragraphs 1 and 2 consolidate and extend students' knowledge of present and perfect forms. They should now learn to recognize regular perfect forms in the 1st, 2nd, and 4th conjugations, and examples of irregular perfects. Follow up with the exercises in paragraphs 3 and 4, and further examples taken from the stories if necessary.

Cultural context material (pp. 174–177)

Content. An account of the destruction of Pompeii in the eruption and the subsequent history of the site.

Suggestions for discussion. Study this section after the Latin stories have been read. It can be used as an observation exercise, with students being led by the teacher's questions to draw their own deductions from the pictures, and to extend them by reference to the text. Possible discussion points:

How do we know that the city came to a sudden end and did not just fade away?

How do archaeologists gather information when they excavate a site?

Given the large population living near Pompeii today (see photograph, p. 173), how would a modern-day eruption compare with the one in our stories?

Further information. Based on three frescoes (one in Herculaneum, two in Pompeii), Vesuvius apparently had only one peak before the AD 79 eruption. From the founding of Pompeii (built on prehistoric lava slopes) by the Oscans in the eighth century BC there had been no volcanic activity and, consequently, no traditional warnings handed down. Descriptions by Diodorus Siculus, Vitruvius, and Strabo indicate that the ancients thought the volcano was extinct. The steep-sided mountain was covered with woods and terraced vineyards that produced the famous Campanian wine. Even the huge crater was filled with vegetation, and it was here that Spartacus and his slave army took refuge. The entire Campanian region was an exceptionally fertile and pleasant area where almost every important Roman family owned property and where luxurious villas and flourishing farms dotted the landscape.

Only Seneca and Tacitus (very briefly) refer to the earthquake of February 5th, AD 62 or 63, that shook the area and caused devastation in Pompeii. Seneca dates it to 63 and Tacitus to 62 (Seneca, *Naturales Quaestiones* VI, 1; Tacitus, *Annales* XV, 22). The series of wax tablets on which Caecilius had recorded his business transactions break off in this year and were stored away in the upper story at the rear of the house.

Caecilius commissioned a new two-panel marble relief for his lararium, one illustrating the north end of the forum, the other portraying the scene at the Porta Vesuvio, not far up the street from where he lived. By AD 79, many public buildings had not yet been repaired and several owners of large villas had subdivided their property. However, Pompeians remained unaware of the danger yet to come.

The story of the final catastrophe at Pompeii and the gradual rediscovery of it has been told in many places. The best contemporary description of the eruption is that of the seventeen-year-old Pliny the Younger, who was at Misenum. One manuscript of Pliny (*Codex Laurentianus Mediceus*) gives the date of the eruption as August 24th but this may be contradicted by archaeological evidence. This latter includes the fact that the people buried in the ashes are wearing heavier clothing than might be expected in August, while the fruit and vegetables in the shops preserved by the ash were those found in October.

Students may have seen pictures from the 1980 eruption of Mt St Helens in Washington State (e.g. *National Geographic Magazine*, January 1981). The most recent research indicates that the AD 79 eruption of Vesuvius, like that of Mt St Helens, was an explosive one (not one with slow-moving lava flows), but was ten times more forceful. In fact, the AD 79 eruption was one of the most disastrous volcanic eruptions in history. Ash and lapilli (small, pebble-sized lava fragments) fell on Rome and on various other Italian cities far from Campania. The extent of the devastation on Pompeii itself can be explained with the help of the map (p. 174). Because of the strength and direction of the wind during the eruption, the super-heated, mushroom-shaped cloud of lapilli and gas collapsed onto Pompeii.

Some people in Pompeii, as well as in Herculaneum and Oplontis, died from the intense heat of the pyroclastic flow. Other possible causes of death were falling masonry, sulphur fumes, and ash asphyxiation.

The students find this Stage fascinating. They will want to know if Vesuvius is still active. The volcano has erupted eighty times since AD 79, most violently in 1631 and 1906. The most recent eruption was in 1944. Students will want to know how many people died. It is as difficult to arrive at such figures as it is to calculate the population of Pompeii at the time. Some archaeologists estimate that up to 10 percent of the population may have perished.

Illustrations

p. 174 • Model showing part of Pompeii as excavated (*Naples, Archaeological Museum*). The diagram shows the features to note:

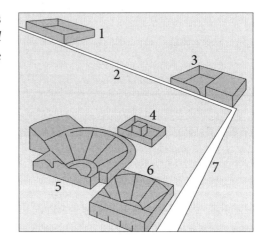

  1   Eumachia's building

  2   The Street of Shops

  3   The Stabian Baths

  4   The temple of Isis in its precinct

  5   The large theater

  6   The small theater

  7   Stabiae Street

• Looking up to a second-floor apartment in Herculaneum. Most of the street frontage has fallen away. Often upper floors contained apartments occupied separately from the first floor, and space was gained, as here, by the upper floor jutting out over the sidewalk. In this room, traces of painted wall decoration can be seen as well as a marble table.

p. 175 • General view of the excavated portion of Herculaneum. In the foreground are some of the large Roman houses on the former seawall. Vesuvius rises in the background above the modern town.

• Eighteenth-century picture of the early excavations from a lavish book, *Campi Phlegraei* (1776), published by the British ambassador to Naples, Sir William Hamilton. Compare the picture with the photograph of the temple of Isis as it is today, p. 169.

p. 176 • A resin cast made on the same principles as the earlier plaster casts. This victim was found in "Villa B" at Oplontis, near Pompeii.

• One of a number of skeletons belonging to people sheltering in the boat houses, created from the supporting arches of the seawall at Herculaneum. The gold wire earrings probably held pearls. Compare the snake's-head bracelets with the one on p. 14. Notice how good her teeth are; she had no cavities because of the local diet of seafood rich in fluoride (*National Geographic Magazine*).

p. 177 • Replanted vineyard in the southeast quarter of Pompeii, largely given over to vineyards and market gardening. The exact pattern of planting was recovered in an excavation by Wilhelmina Jashemsky. The vineyard contained an outdoor triclinium where the owner and his guests could enjoy the wine from the crop.

• A group of casts huddled in a corner of the same vineyard. The crawling child on p. 171 belongs to this group.

p. 178 A lantern, *in situ* in the House of Menander, Pompeii. Instead of glass, it would originally have had a thin sheet of horn to protect the flame.

Suggestions for further activities

1 Research projects on the geophysics of eruptions, or the phenomena of this eruption, or a study of another modern eruption.
2 Draw individual pictures or class murals depicting the scene in Pompeian streets or in the forum during the eruption.
3 Prepare an audio or video news report describing the final hours of Pompeii, complete with appropriately horrific sound effects.
4 Make a plaster or papier-mâché cast based on one made in Pompeii.

Vocabulary checklist (p. 178)

fundus gives us "fundamental," since it also means *bottom, base*.

The English word "tandem," referring to riding bicycles, horses, etc. behind one another, is actually a pun on the old-fashioned translation *at length* for the Latin word **tandem**.

Language information

About the language (pp. 182–190)

This section provides a reference and review for students. It collects and organizes various grammatical features, such as the cases of nouns and the persons and tenses of verbs. It also amplifies certain grammatical points from the students' readings.

The exercises in these notes are to be used at whatever point in Unit 1 you believe students can most usefully, confidently, and successfully complete them, probably after Stage 8. They can serve as a model for further exercises which teachers could compose. You may also find them suitable as a review of first-year grammar when beginning the second year of Latin study. Such exercises are more effective in developing comprehension skills than memorization of isolated paradigm charts.

Illustration

p. 179 Mosaic of guard dog at entrance to the House of the Tragic Poet, opposite the Forum Baths, Pompeii. Inscription reads **CAVE CANEM**, "Beware of the dog."

Vocabulary (pp. 191–201)

This section is a cumulated vocabulary for the entire Unit. Its format and content are explained in notes on pp. 191–192 of the students' textbook. If you wish to give students a formal introduction to this section by discussing the notes, consider waiting until at least Stage 2, when the concepts of nominative and accusative are introduced, before discussing paragraphs 1–3; and Stage 7, when the format of presenting the perfect tense is introduced, before discussing paragraphs 4–7.

Linguistic synopsis of Unit 1

The following synopsis indicates the chief linguistic features introduced in each Stage; it also shows whether each feature is described and/or practiced in the current Stage or a later one and/or the Language information (LI) section for Unit 1. All features not described in the Unit 1 Language information section will be described in the Language information sections of later Units.

You can use the synopsis to:

1 Check whether a feature occurring in a Stage's reading material is newly introduced in that Stage.
2 Discover where a particular feature is discussed.
3 Find out the Stage in which a particular feature first occurs.

In addition to the traditional grammatical categories of morphology and syntax, the synopsis includes some of the chief sentence patterns of Unit 1, printed in capital letters. These are not normally discussed in the Stage language notes, but examples are collected under the heading Word order in the Language information section in this and subsequent Units. When you make up extra sentences to practice a language point, it is important that the word order of those sentences should follow a pattern which students have already met; the synopsis is often helpful here.

When reading a Stage with a class, concentrate on the features dealt with in that Stage's language note, rather than attempt to discuss every feature listed here.

Stage	Linguistic feature	Place of language note etc.
1	word order with and without **est**	1
	nominative singular	2
2	nominative (met in Stage 1) and accusative singular	2, LI
	superlative	8
	NOMINATIVE + ACCUSATIVE + VERB word order	LI
3	nominative and accusative of 1st, 2nd, and 3rd declensions	3, LI
	attributive adjective (predicative adjective met in Stage 1)	14, 18
	VERB + NOMINATIVE word order	
4	1st and 2nd person singular present (including **sum**)	4, LI
	mē	9
	questions with **quis, quid, cūr, ubi**	11
	questions with no interrogative word	11
	adest	
5	nominative plural	5, LI
	3rd person plural present	5, LI
	two nominatives joined by **et**	LI
	puer	
	abest	

6	3rd person singular and plural, imperfect and perfect (**v-** stems)	6, LI
	erat and **erant**	6, LI
	clauses with **postquam** and **quod**	LI
	two accusatives joined with **et**	LI
	clauses with **ubi** (= *where*)	
7	ACCUSATIVE + VERB word order (i.e. subject omitted)	7, LI
	perfect tense (other than **v-** stems)	7, LI
	tē	9
	oblique cases of **is**	Unit 2
8	accusative plural	8, LI
	superlative (met from Stage 2)	8
	hic	19
9	dative singular and plural	9, LI
	nominative, accusative, and dative of **ego** and **tū**	9
	NOMINATIVE + DATIVE + ACCUSATIVE + VERB word order	LI
	ille	19
	ferō	
10	1st and 2nd person plural present (including **sum**)	10, LI
	comparative adjective	10
	comparison with **quam**	10
	nōbīs and **vōbīs**	11
	questions with **-ne**	11
	imperative singular	19
	two datives joined with **et**	LI
	in + accusative (two examples)	
	eō	
11	intransitive verbs + dative	11
	placet	11
	questions with	
	quis, **quid** etc. (met from Stage 4)	
	no interrogative word (from Stage 4)	
	-ne (from Stage 10)	11
	nōbīs and **vōbīs**	11
	vocative	19
	NOMINATIVE + DATIVE + VERB word order	
	mēcum and **tēcum**	
12	1st and 2nd person singular and plural, imperfect and perfect	12, LI
	1st and 2nd person singular and plural imperfect of **esse**	12, LI
	postquam clauses containing DATIVE + ACCUSATIVE + VERB	
	word order	
	ablative plural in prepositional phrases	

The following terms are introduced in Unit 1. Numerals indicate the Stage in which each term is first used. LI = Language information section.

Term	Stage
noun	2
case	2
nominative	2
accusative	2
declension	3
verb	4
singular	5
plural	5
tense	6
present	6
imperfect	6
perfect	6
superlative	8
dative	9
comparative	10
preposition	LI
conjugation	LI
irregular	LI
conjunction	LI

Appendix A: Diagnostic tests

The tests below are designed not to measure achievement but to diagnose students' progress and to determine, at periodic intervals, the degree to which they have understood recent material, have integrated less recent material into their understanding, need review of grammar, or need drill on basic vocabulary. They also give students useful practice in working unaided.

Supply students with a typed copy of the story and ask them to write an English translation. In the tests, the words and phrases in **boldface** are either new to students or have appeared infrequently in the Stages. You might provide meanings for these words, since most students are unlikely to recognize words they have seen only once or twice previously.

The tests are not designed to provide a good grade curve. From the teacher's viewpoint, the total number of points earned by each student is less important than his or her performance in specific sections. Resist, however, the impulse to review intensively areas in which students show themselves, on these diagnostic tests, to be weak. More properly, incorporate such review into your lesson plans over a span of weeks.

When correcting the tests, keep the following points in mind:

1   Any English translation that faithfully reflects the meaning of the Latin is acceptable. Structural equivalence should not be insisted upon.

2   Do not take off an excessive number of points if students mistake the meaning or inflection of words with which they have not long been familiar.

3   Students will probably have most difficulty with sentences that show a strong contrast with English structure (e.g. sentences with subject omitted).

Where students have difficulty, it i s sometimes useful to refer them to familiar sentences that illustrate the point causing them difficulty (the model sentences are often suitable for this purpose). Then make up further examples for students to translate.

Test 1

To be given to pupils after Stage 4 has been completed.

ad carcerem

iūdex Hermogenem **convincit**.

"ego Hermogenem **ad carcerem mittō**," inquit iūdex.

"ego sum **innocēns**," clāmat Hermogenēs.

"**immō**, tū es mercātor **scelestus**!" respondet iūdex. "tū **multam** pecūniam dēbēs."

servus mercātōrem scelestum ē **basilicā trahit**. servus mercātōrem ad carcerem dūcit et iānuam **pulsat**. **custōs** iānuam **aperit**. custōs est Grōma. Grōma mercātōrem **statim agnōscit**. Grōma rīdet.

"Hermogenēs est amīcus **veterrimus**," inquit Grōma. "Hermogenēs vīllam nōn habet. Hermogenēs in carcere **habitat**!"

servus rīdet. sed Hermogenēs nōn rīdet. Hermogenēs Grōmam vituperat. Grōma est īrātus. Grōma mercātōrem ad carcerem trahit.

"**cella tua** est **parāta**," inquit Grōma.

Test 2

To be given at the end of Stage 8.

vīlla scelesta

in urbe erat vīlla pulchra. vīlla tamen erat **vacua**, quod **umbra ibi** habitābat. omnēs **cīvēs** umbram valdē timēbant.

Athēnodōrus ad urbem vēnit et **dē umbrā** audīvit. Athēnodōrus tamen umbrās nōn timēbat, quod erat **philosophus**. vīllam igitur **ēmit**.

postquam **nox** vēnit, Athēnodōrus in ātriō sedēbat. subitō philosophus **fragōrem** audīvit. **respexit** et umbram **horribilem** vīdit. umbra erat senex et multās **catēnās gerēbat**. umbra, postquam **ingemuit**, ad hortum **lentē** ambulābat. Athēnodōrus quoque ad hortum ambulāvit. postquam Athēnodōrus hortum intrāvit, umbra subitō **ēvānuit**.

tum Athēnodōrus servōs vocāvit. servī **pālās** portāvērunt et hortum intrāvērunt. servī, postquam in hortō **fōdērunt**, **hominem** mortuum **invēnērunt**.

Athēnodōrus hominem **rītē sepelīvit**, quod philosophus erat **benignus**. Athēnodōrus umbram **numquam** iterum vīdit.

Test 3

To be given during or at the end of Stage 12.

Caecilius et Phormiō

ōlim mercātor diem nātālem celebrābat. mercātor Caecilium ad cēnam invītāvit. Caecilius cum servō ad vīllam contendit, ubi mercātor habitābat. servus erat Phormiō. Caecilius, postquam vīllam intrāvit, multōs amīcōs vīdit. cēna amīcōs valdē dēlectāvit. omnēs multum vīnum bibēbant et multās fābulās nārrābant. tandem ē vīllā discessērunt. Caecilius et Phormiō quoque discessērunt. viae erant **dēsertae**, quod omnēs Pompēiānī dormiēbant.

trēs fūrēs tamen per viās **errābant**. fūrēs, postquam Caecilium cōnspexērunt, dīxērunt,

"ecce! Caecilius adest. Caecilius est argentārius et multam pecūniam habet."

fūrēs Caecilium ferōciter pulsābant. Caecilium ad **terram dēiēcērunt**. Phormiō tamen ad fūrēs **sē praecipitāvit** et omnēs superāvit. Caecilius postquam **convaluit**, Phormiōnem **līberāvit**. Caecilius Phormiōnī pecūniam dedit, quod **fidēlis** erat.

Appendix B: Select bibliography

A few books are out of print (OP) but are included in case teachers already possess them or can obtain secondhand copies.

Where to start

Aldrete, G. S. *Daily Life in the Roman City: Rome, Pompeii, and Ostia* (Greenwood Press, 2004)

Beard, M. *The Fires of Vesuvius: Pompeii Lost and Found* (Harvard University Press, 2008)

Berry, J. *The Complete Pompeii* (Thames & Hudson, 2007)

Carcopino, J. *Daily Life in Ancient Rome* (Penguin, 1991)

Clarke, J. R. *Roman Life* (Abrams, 2007)

Cooley, A.E. & Cooley, M.G.L. *Pompeii and Herculaneum: A Sourcebook* (Routledge, 2014)

Roberts, P. *Life and Death in Pompeii and Herculaneum* (British Museum Press, 2013)

Shelton, J. *As the Romans Did: A Sourcebook in Roman Social History* (Oxford University Press, 1997)

Pompeii and Herculaneum

Allison, P. M. *Pompeian Households: An Analysis of the Material Culture* (Cotsen Institute of Archaeology Press, 2004)

Brown, D., ed. *Pompeii: The Vanished City* (Time Life Books, 1992)

Dobbins, J.J. & Foss, P. *The World of Pompeii* (Routledge, 2007)

Grant, M. *Cities of Vesuvius* (Penguin, 1976) (OP)

Jacobelli, K. *Gladiators at Pompeii* (J. Paul Getty Museum, 2004)

Ling, R. *Pompeii: History, Life and Afterlife* (Tempus, 2005)

Wallace-Hadrill, A. *Houses and Society in Pompeii and Herculaneum* (Princeton University Press, 1994)

Wallace-Hadrill, A. *Herculaneum: Past and Future* (Frances Lincoln, 2011)

Zanker, P. *Pompeii: Public and Private Life* (Harvard University Press, 1999)

Site guides and exhibition catalogs:

Art and History of Pompeii (Bonechi Guides, 1997)

de Caro, S. *The National Archaeological Museum of Naples* (Electa Napoli, 1996)

de Franciscis, A. *Pompeii, Monuments Past and Present* (Interdipress, 1995) (Available on site.)

Guzzo, P. G. *Pompeii: Guide to the Site* (Electa Napoli, 2002)

Mattusch, C. C., ed. *Pompeii and the Roman Villa: Art and Culture around the Bay of Naples* (National Gallery of Art, Washington, 2009)

Roman society

Clarke, J. R. *Art in the Lives of Ordinary Romans: Visual Representation and Non-Elite Viewers in Italy, 100 BC–AD 315* (University of California Press, 2003)

Giardina, A., ed. *The Romans* (University of Chicago Press, 1993) (Essays on such topics as "The Soldier," "The Slave, The Freedman," "The Merchant," etc.)

Isaac, B. *The Invention of Racism in Classical Antiquity* (Princeton University Press, 2004)

Jones, P. & Sidwell, K., eds *The World of Rome: An Introduction to Roman Culture* (Cambridge University Press, 1997)

Kamm, A. *The Romans: An Introduction* (Routledge, 1995)

Knapp, R. *Invisible Romans* (Profile Books, 2013)

Rawson, B., ed. *A Companion to Families in the Greek and Roman Worlds* (Blackwell, 2010)

Rawson, B. & Weaver, P. *The Roman Family in Italy: Status, Sentiment, Space* (Oxford Clarendon Press, 1997)

Snowden, F. *Before Color Prejudice: The Ancient View of Blacks* (Harvard University Press, 1991)

Toner, J. *Popular Culture in Ancient Rome* (Polity, 2009)

Women

Fantham, E., et al. *Women in the Classical World: Images and Text* (Oxford University Press, 1994)

Lefkowitz, M.R. & Fant, M.B., eds *Women's Life in Greece and Rome: A Sourcebook in Translation* (Johns Hopkins University Press, 1992)

Leisure and entertainment

Beacham, R. *The Roman Theatre and its Audience* (Harvard University Press, 1996)

Bomgardner, D. L. *The Story of the Roman Amphitheatre* (Routledge, 2002)

Dunbabin, K.M.D. *The Roman Banquet: Images of Conviviality* (Cambridge University Press, 2007)

McLeish, K. *Food and Drink (Greek & Roman Topics)* (Collins, 1978)

Toner, J. *Leisure and Ancient Rome* (Polity, 2013)

Slavery

Bradley, K.R. *Slaves and Masters in the Roman Empire: A Study in Social Control* (Oxford University Press, 1987)

Bradley, K.R. *Slavery and Society at Rome* (Cambridge University Press, 1994)

Toner, J. *The Roman Guide to Slave Management* (The Overlook Press, 2014)

Education

Barrow, R. *Greek and Roman Education* (Duckworth, 1996)

Bonner, S.F. *Education in Ancient Rome* (Bristol Classical Press, 1977)

Books for students

Amery, H. & Vanags, P. *The Time Traveller Book of Rome and the Romans* (Usborne, 1993)

Andrews, I. *Pompeii* (Cambridge University Press, 1978)

Bisel, S. *The Secrets of Vesuvius* (Random House, 1990) (OP)

Carpiceci, A. *Pompeii Nowadays and 2000 Years Ago* (Bonechi, 1977)

Connolly, P. *Pompeii* (Oxford University Press, 1990) (Highly recommended.)

Connolly, P. & Dodge, H. *Ancient City: Life in Classical Athens & Rome* (Oxford University Press, 1998)

Deem, J. M. *Bodies from the Ash: Life and Death in Ancient Pompeii* (HMH Books for Younger Readers, 2005)

Deiss, J.J. *Herculaneum: Italy's Buried Treasure* (J. Paul Getty Museum, 1995)

Etienne, R. *Pompeii – The Day a City Died* (Abrams, 1992)

Hicks, P. *Pompeii and Herculaneum* (Thomson Learning/Wayland Publishing, 1996)

Humphrey, K.L. *Pompeii, Nightmare at Midday* (Watts Books, 1995)

James, S. *Eyewitness Books: Ancient Rome* (Stoddart, 1990)

Macaulay, D. *City: A Story of Roman Planning and Construction* (Houghton Mifflin, 1974)

Malam, J. *You Wouldn't Want to Live in Pompeii! A Volcanic Eruption You'd Rather Avoid* (Franklin Watts, 2008)

Malam, J. *You Wouldn't Want to Be a Roman Gladiator!* (Franklin Watts, 2012)

Matyszak, P. *Ancient Rome on Five Denarii a Day* (Thames and Hudson, 2007)

Matyszak, P. *Gladiator: The Roman Fighter's (Unofficial) Manual* (Thames and Hudson, 2011)

McLeish, K. *Roman Comedy* (Duckworth, 1986)

Sonneborn, L. *Pompeii (Unearthing Ancient Worlds)* (Twenty-First Century Books, 2008)

Watkins, R. *Gladiator* (Houghton Mifflin, 1997)

Historical novels

Davis, L. *Shadows in Bronze* (Ballantine, 1992) (The author has written a series of detective novels set in the time of Vespasian. The Bay of Naples area is the setting for *Shadows in Bronze*.)

Dillon, E. *The Shadow of Vesuvius* (Faber, 1978) (OP)

Harris, R. *Pompeii* (Random House, 2005)

Lawrence, C. *The Thieves of Ostia* (Orion Children's Books, 2002) (The *Roman Mysteries* series includes seventeen books and follows the adventures of four children who solve mysteries in the Bay of Naples, Rome, Greece, and beyond in the time of Titus.)

Sontag, S. *The Volcano Lover: A Romance* (Farrar Straus and Giroux, 1992) (The story of Sir William Hamilton and his interest in Vesuvius and the antiquities of Pompeii.)

Wilson, B.K. *Beloved of the Gods* (Constable, 1965) (OP)